Better Than We Believed

Better Than We Believed

How to Apply the Vision That Is Faith
to the Struggle That Is Life

by
Robert J. Cormier

A Crossroad Book
The Crossroad Publishing Company
New York

The Crossroad Publishing Company
www.CrossroadPublishing.com

Printed in the United States of America in 2013.

ISBN 978-08245-49800 (alk. paper)

Library of Congress Cataloging-in-Publication Data available from the Library of Congress.

Cover design by George Foster

In continuation of our 200-year tradition of independent publishing, The Crossroad Publishing Company proudly offers a variety of books with strong, original voices and diverse perspectives. The viewpoints expressed in our books are not necessarily those of The Crossroad Publishing Company, any of its imprints or of its employees. No claims are made or responsibility assumed for any health or other benefit.

Books published by The Crossroad Publishing Company may be purchased at special quantity discount rates for classes and institutional use. For information, please e-mail sales@CrossroadPublishing.com.

CONTENTS

CONTENTS

PART IV: EIGHT MORE STORIES

◨

INTRODUCTION

Life, most people will say, is not easy.

For many of us, much of the time, there is a lot of work that is rarely rewarded, or even appreciated, as much as we think it should be.

For many of us, some of the time, there is real pain in the constant distance between what we want from life and what we have, or ever will have.

Then, there is the almost constant battle with insecurity, especially around people who are good-looking or especially talented or rich, or bosses, or people everyone else seems to admire.

We suffer many slights, carry a number of unhappy memories, and, looking ahead, often we have to fight off an assortment of fears.

Then there are the big things. Sooner or later, in almost everyone's life, some really serious things have to be dealt with. Sometimes there is more than one such thing at once.

In all these cases, faith is supposed to help. We hear it all the time.

But faith in what exactly? That God will save me from my problems? Is this, really, what I expect? Is it usually what I see?

If not, then faith in what?

And, if I hear about something interesting and uplifting, how do I know that this is not just wishful thinking?

And, if I have reason to believe that faith in something specific is not just wishful thinking, how does this faith change things — especially the big things?

The best way to understand how faith changes things is to see it happen.

In the pages ahead, in Part I of this little book, you are going to meet seven people with made-up names whose struggles are very real.

They represent the problems of many, many people in our modern world, people who were not given a very compelling idea of what faith really is. But this is precisely what they need.

These characters have one experience in common: each goes to hear a spiritual talk entitled "Faith: We Have It Backwards!"

What the presenter of this talk actually has in mind is a forward-looking view of faith. He is very aware that his audience, and the rest of us, hear about matters of faith and the meaning of life from many people, many of whom seem sure and speak well, and yet so much of what we hear contradicts. This makes it hard for us to feel confident about what to believe.

Presuming nothing, the presenter will try to show his listeners how to experience God for themselves, and from this experience to derive an explanation of life that makes so much sense they can hardly imagine that it *isn't* true!

He will then try to show how this explanation of life changes the way we see everything, including everything we struggle with, and gives us an inner peace, purpose, and joy we might never have imagined.

In the wake of this talk, Part II of this book, all seven decide to seek an appointment with the presenter.

In the stories about these appointments, Part III of this book, faith is applied to their problems in ways they never expected.

Perhaps, by watching it done, you will learn how to apply faith to any similar problem, including the problems of people around you.

Part IV will offer "Eight More Stories" involving issues important to many and wisdom allied to faith. I hope there will be something here that you or someone you know can use.

In any case, you may find that things are better than you believed and now you believe in a better way. ∎

PART I:
RECOGNIZE ANYONE?

■

MARK
(STRUGGLES WITH ANGER)

Mark had been angry for so long that he thought it was normal.

But Mark had not always been angry. In fact, he had had a relatively happy childhood. He came from a nice family that went through its "moments," but nothing was too traumatic. His folks were good providers, and they provided Mark and his brother and sisters with a home and the other modern necessities: some discipline, some religion, a sufficient number of toys, and time to be kids.

Of course, the kids spent a lot of time watching television, but they did other things too, and they had fun, and they had dreams.

Mark's dream was typical for his age and time. He was going to play football. He was going to be a quarterback. He was going to win the Super Bowl.

The dream died quietly as it does for almost everyone. Usually by the time you *don't* make it to the next level you already know you're not going to be the greatest ever. Since nobody but you was expecting this, there isn't much embarrassment; and your parents wanted you to be realistic anyway.

You could still have a dream with a girl, and "the good life" that was supposed to come with things that cost money.

In the case of the girl, her name was Karen; and if she was not the kind that others ogle, she was the prettiest and nicest girl who was interested in Mark.

The money would come from a job. Since Mark was not especially interested in any particular career, college seemed pointless, time-consuming, and too expensive. Mark knew somebody at a distribution business; he could start in the warehouse and move up to the front office, and he would make money.

He did move up and made more money, and he married Karen, and not long thereafter they were expecting their first child. This seemed to be a very good thing to be doing with one's life.

Mark was there for the birth of his son; and mother and child did fine.

Being new parents was interesting, scary, tiring, and sometimes fun. Karen and Mark raised their little boy through a couple of phases; figured that things would go even more smoothly the second time around, and decided to have another child. This time it was a girl, and that was good. Things did go more smoothly, but now they decided that enough was enough and, anyway, there were plenty of parenting challenges ahead.

Meanwhile, Mark continued to go to work. This was never fun, and with time it became even less so. It was mostly routine, and this meant it was boring. Too often it seemed that it was necessary to make a big deal out of something that really wasn't important. And other people didn't make things any easier. Too often they were careless; sometimes they were nasty. Days were long.

Besides all this, Mark had a boss. Mark was an adult and still he had someone telling him what to do.

All of this was wearing on Mark, making him feel "old" even though he was only in his 30s. He seemed locked into a certain kind of life and he did not like it.

In his growing frustration, Mark decided to break out. He would go into business on his own. He knew the business. He had many contacts. People liked him. He would be his own boss. He would start out small but that was OK. He would make it. Who knew how far he could go?

He didn't go very far. Every time he thought he was getting somewhere something unexpected set him back.

He tried branching out into this. More work, not much to show for it.

He tried investing in that. And almost lost his shirt.

He wanted to try something else. But this was for insiders only and he was not "in."

Of course, every setback made him more angry. Every long, hard day made things a little worse. "I just can't get a break," he said, "life is not fair."

He drank some, but this was not the problem. He was often cranky and short with the kids, but he was not abusive. He was just unhappy.

That's what Karen said when she heard about a fairly well-known speaker talker who was coming to a church they went to fairly often. He was giving a talk called "Faith: We Have It Backwards!" It was supposed to be about how faith can make you happy, or something like that.

"It's one night," said Karen, "what can it hurt?"

Mark agreed to go. ∎

■

IRENE
(IS REALLY STRESSED)

Irene was one of those people whose days seemed to connect. She was barely done for the day when it was time for bed. She was so tired that she fell asleep immediately. The next thing she knew it was another day with very many things to do.

All of this was a labor of love. Irene loved her family very much, almost to a fault. The fault was the feeling that as much as she was doing it was never enough.

Irene often worried about her family. For no reason that she could put into words, she feared that "something" could go wrong.

For Irene, worrying, *not* really being at peace, was not a new feeling. Even from childhood Irene was almost conscious of anxiety.

It's not that she came from hardship. Her family was not poor; her parents didn't fight a lot. But they did expect a lot from her. And didn't they always have something to say!? "Don't do it that way." "You could do better." "Boy, that other girl is smart… pretty… really talented…."

Irene was a good person — no one ever said otherwise — but was she *very* good? Was she someone that made a big impression on other people? Was it so wrong that she wanted to be?

Oh, sometimes it appeared that her parents were proud of her. Once or twice they even said so. But this was when everyone is expected to be proud for something that almost everybody does, like graduate, get a job, round-number birthdays.

Irene did have good friends—she was a good friend—but even with them she was not always comfortable. They didn't make a lot of comparisons, at least not out loud, but Irene did—at least in her mind, and she often felt that she came out at the low end of most measures.

She often thought that others were looking back at her. This is what others do, isn't it? They're there, they see, and when a person makes a mistake, or doesn't know something, or is simply not cool, they notice. It happens all the time.

Life brought Irene together with Vinnie, a good guy. Vinnie appreciated Irene, except when he didn't get his way. Then he didn't appreciate her so much; and this was hard on Irene, and she tried not to let it happen too often.

Motherhood made Irene feel that she had accomplished something. But it also made her nervous. So many things could go wrong. If something happened to one of the kids…she just couldn't bear to think about that.

Nor could she afford to be fully conscious of her fear that the kids would *do* wrong. How would we handle that?! And what would everyone think!?

Life was not easy but Irene did not expect it to be easy. When was it ever easy? Maybe it wasn't so tough for everyone—certainly it seemed that others had it easier, and had a better life—but this was her life and where could she go for another?

What got her thinking was an announcement at church. "Do you often feel agitated inside for no good reason?" it asked. "Do you ever feel that you are really at peace?" The announcement also said that peace was possible. "This is what faith wants for you. Maybe it has not been working because 'We Have It Backwards.' Come and see."

This was another thing that Irene felt that she should do. So of course, she would do it. ■

□

HENRY
(IS BEING CONSUMED BY HATRED)

Henry had hardly been a saint, but it never occurred to him that somebody would do something like this to him. How had he deserved it?

All he wanted was to be a success.

He had done well-enough in school. Gotten his degree. Got into a big company. Found out that his degree had not at all prepared him for what he was expected to do. Set about learning the ropes. Did his best.

He did what was expected and more. He had ideas; he took initiative; he followed through.

Henry was doing well, and he attracted the attention of the big bosses. This, however, was perceived by his immediate supervisor, who realized that Henry was becoming his competition for a major job that was soon to become open. So his supervisor went to work—on Henry.

At first, Henry did not realize that he was being sent out of the plant for trivial errands—almost every day. But, he thought, you don't impress people by complaining about your work.

This was part of the reason he was so surprised when his periodic review was shown to him. While it didn't outright accuse him of anything, it was written in a way that insinuated mediocrity at every turn, going so far as to suggest that the more we know Henry the less impressed we are. (Was this a way to get around the good reviews that Henry had always gotten in the past?)

By now, Henry was suspicious, and so it did not shock him when some of his coworkers came to him out of friendship.

"That guy is out to get you," one said, "he used to talk about how slow you were; but now he's starting to make it sound as though you're stealing."

"He told one of the big bosses that he 'thought' you came back from the printers drunk."

Henry had to do something. So he confronted his supervisor who, of course, denied everything. He tried to make it sound as though Henry's coworkers were the ones out to get him.

But Henry knew better. He knew who his friends were; and he could spot a phony.

He tried to get a word with one of the big bosses. But there was little time for Henry, and he knew he had not been listened to. The damage was done, he thought, and it was too late.

Henry's supervisor got the promotion he was after. After that, he paid little attention to Henry. Now that Henry was no longer a threat, his old boss was almost friendly.

But Henry could not take it. He knew what had happened, and he thought about it all day long.

Days went by and time only made things worse.

Before long, he could take it no longer, and he left that company.

He got another job, an OK job, but still he could not stop thinking about what had happened at the old job. He got madder and madder.

Henry got so angry that he could not enjoy anything. He was torturing those around him because he could not stop talking about it. At times he even imagined himself doing violence. He had never felt this way before.

Perhaps this is why he was open to something he had never done before — going to a lecture in a church. It was called "Faith: We Have It Backwards!" Henry did not know what this meant, but he hoped he would hear about how the good would be rewarded and the evil would get theirs. ∎

□

GLORIA
(HAS BEEN BETRAYED)

Gloria saw it coming. Her marriage began as well as most, then started to fade with the newness, and endured afterward out of inertia — a combination of no real problems, a sense of rightness, and a resistance to change.

This, however, was not a good basis for companionship, and for years now the relatively superficial companionship with which they started had devolved into watching TV together most nights during the week.

Of course, this was not much of a hedge against temptation, especially when Charlie turned 50. He worked with various younger women. One was bound to be needy of attention — and good at giving it. He started down the slippery slope.

When things really started happening Charlie was clumsy and there were plenty of signs. Gloria saw them, asked some questions, accepted his vaguely plausible answers, and started to live in doubt.

It did not take long for more questions to provoke fights, and it did not take long for the fights to give Charlie his excuse to get out. He admitted nothing, did not think there was any point to getting help — he did not need help; she needed "to get off his back" — and soon after this he announced that he was moving out "to be on his own."

Gloria was alternately hurt, angry, scared, and embarrassed.

It got worse when people starting seeing Charlie and "that skinny girl" here and there, and what Gloria suspected was now confirmed. There seemed little to talk about after that.

The divorce was quick because he conceded her as much as he could. You could tell, he did feel a little guilty, but this was no consolation, none at all.

She did know that she must still go on for the sake of her two children. And she also knew that she felt…the only word that came to her was "empty." This was when she was not hurt, angry, scared, or embarrassed. Worst of all, she did not know what to think about the rest of her life.

This was what made her open to something at church. She could not make much sense of the topic, "Faith: We Have It Backwards!" but she could use a night out and the company of her friend Irene, who was already going. ▪

◘

MARY
(FEELS TRAPPED BY HER DUTY TO A LOVED ONE)

Mary had not expected this. Maybe she should have. After all, things happen; in time they are almost sure to happen; and in couples they usually happen first to men.

The problem is worse when there are no physical symptoms.

When the problem is something going on invisibly inside someone's head, it's harder not to blame him. If only you could see something wrong, it would be easier to act understanding. At least, that's what Mary told herself—and others.

Dave and Mary had been married for a long time. They stopped thinking about *how* long when for them "married life" became synonymous with "life."

It was a good life. They did not think "great" life; and certainly there were some difficult moments; and there were many minor irritations ("why does he never do this, why does she always talk about that"), but, in sum, it was a good life.

It was a good life, and it was getting ready to move into a new phase—retirement. The kids, of course, were long gone and doing fine. Money was not a problem, and there was still some energy. Maybe now they could travel a bit, finally take up gardening (or, in his case…he would find something), and just take life easier.

Not long after the work-a-day pressures were lifted from Dave's head, his mind began to slip. Of course, it was subtle at first, forgetting things, doing things backwards, eating at odd hours. But then he starting doing all sorts of things, pointless things, at odd hours. And it was getting harder and harder to reason with him. He was never nasty; that was not his style; but he just didn't get it, or if he did, he would soon forget it. Mary was the one getting nasty.

She started to get scared when he left the water in the sink running, and went out and left the door open, and when he got home he could not remember where he had been.

There were appointments with doctors, of course. There must be *something* that could be done. And even though something was done — if you go to doctors, they have to do *something* — it didn't really help, and it wasn't really expected to.

This was not how Mary had envisioned the next phase of her life. It was not fun and not fair.

It was the unfairness of it all that bothered Mary most.

Life had rarely been all that much fun. A mother's work is never done; she learned this quickly. Even celebrations meant work, even vacations.

And through it all she did her duty. She (and Dave) played by the rules. They were helpful to others. They took some responsibility for the kids' activities, doing something for other people's kids. They went to church. They prayed.

Mary was praying now but got no results.

Instead, slowly, Dave was getting worse.

The kids tried to help but, if Mary was not ready to "put" Dave somewhere, there wasn't much they could do.

Even for brief breaks, all too brief breaks, it was all on Mary. It was hard. It was embarrassing. And Mary also felt guilty because it was embarrassing. This made the situation also confusing.

But Mary knew, for sure, that she was angry. And she was conscious enough of herself to know that she was angry at God, and faithful enough to know that this was not good. This made her open to something spiritual. Her friend Joy invited her to a talk at their church. ■

JOY
(CAN'T GET OVER A LOVED ONE'S DEATH)

Joy and Dan had been married for a long time.

They had enjoyed together a more than average happiness, and through hard work raised several children whom they were more than a little proud of.

Then Dan got sick. At first, it didn't seem serious, just something to look into. It still didn't seem too serious. Then it got worse. They were sent to a specialist. It was serious. They did everything they could. There were moments of hope, setbacks, and the final turn for the worse.

Joy was supported through it all, before, during, and after. The kids, especially, did a lot. They came; they helped with the decisions. Afterwards, they got her out; they called.

Nonetheless, Joy had a huge hole in her life. It was there in the morning; it was there at night. There were countless times when she wanted to tell Dan something and had to remember again that he was dead.

Eating alone was awful.

She did go out a bit, as much as she might have wanted to. And some of her friends were in the same boat. They even talked about it; and they talked about a boat, about taking a cruise.

Nonetheless the hole was there; it was always there. A lifetime of relating to someone, of building your identity on your relationship to someone, and now….

This was her thinking on *good* days. Bad days involved doubts and almost unspeakable fears. Where is Dan now? Is he OK? Could he be gone?

Gone…what is "gone"? Joy could barely grasp the question. Could it be that this person, who was a *person*, whom she knew *so* well, no longer existed in any way at all?

Sometimes she cried *for him*, for him thinking of all he had lost.

And forever? For-EVER?!

Then when she realized that she was facing the same fate herself…that was much too much to think about for long. During the few seconds the idea rolled around in her mind, it was too terrible to put into words.

Joy knew that her doubts and fears involved faith. This made her eager when she heard about something coming to her church, something about "basic" faith; she knew that this was what she needed. She called her friend Mary and asked her to go. ■

■

JAMES
(KNOWS HE IS DYING)

Dying caught James by surprise.

Probably this happens to everyone. After all, throughout your life it is *other* people who die.

Yet, James might have known better. He was smart. He was one of the best-educated people he knew. Like other intellectuals whom he knew, he was proud of his objectivity. You don't just believe what you want to. You go with the facts. You are guided by reason (whatever that actually means).

Going by the facts should have meant recognizing that death comes for everyone.

And one might think that recognizing this would affect how one would see life, and live it.

But James had managed to spend his life NOT thinking about it.

Now he had no choice. The symptoms started as no big deal. They were easily mistaken for something minor. They got worse. Now there were tests. The results weren't good. There were treatments that could be tried, but they almost never worked. But James signed up for them anyway. And there was no sign that they were working. The end was not imminent, but it was coming.

Of course, his family was upset. Joan, his wife was really upset; and so it wasn't really possible to talk with her about how he was really feeling.

They did not have kids. (It was supposed to be the thing to do; but why, really? You become the prisoner of kids; but why, really — so that someday *they* can be become the prisoner of kids…?) Now, sometimes, James was consciously happy he didn't have kids — more people to leave behind. Sometimes he wished he did have kids so that he would leave some trace of himself when he passed.

When he was with people, talking about almost anything, James was distracted and got relief. Even if talked about his condition, he found that he rose to the occasion and felt almost brave.

When he was alone, especially during the day, he was struck often by hard thoughts: "How many more times will I see this?" (The leaves changing.) "It looks like I'll never get there." (China.) Stuff like that.

The hardest time was at night.

At night it was hard not to think about the eternal dark. "Is this it? Is this where I am going? I am going nowhere, to be nothing, not to exist, never again, NEVER?"

If he could stop it by screaming…but that would change nothing.

To face it bravely…was that something to be proud of? "Why? I will still die. I, me, will not be anything anymore for-EVER!"

"How can anyone be OK with this?"

James wanted, somehow, to stop time, to hold on to life while he still had it, and not just watch himself irresistibly, irrevocably pass away.

"God, there has to be more to life than this!" James did not recognize that he was praying. But he began to hope for a new truth. And somehow he knew that there was no place to go for it, except back toward the old truth, which he had learned as a boy and quickly "grown out of."

James felt desperate, confused, and even guilty. He had never faced up to a variety of his faults, had hardly ever said that he was sorry, and wouldn't even return the calls of that guy he had sort of swindled.

In the midst of all this inner turmoil, James saw a banner in the front of a church. It was advertising something about faith, and promising peace and joy.

James was desperate. He had to do something; he would go to this talk. ∎

PART II:
FAITH

◨

FAITH: WE HAVE IT BACKWARDS!

For the most part, those who came to "Faith: We Have It Backwards!" were relieved. The hall was relatively filled with other people. No one wants to be the only one, or one of only a few.

The hall was clean and neat; refreshments had been prepared; and there was plenty of light. There were no screens, only a modest podium.

The program began on time, with a prayer by Father Ed, and the explanation that he had invited his friend Father Mike, "because I think we needed something new."

Father Mike got polite applause and off he went. "Thank you so much for coming," he said. "I had to hope that the title of my talk would be more intriguing than insulting." This got a laugh. "But I think you'll see that all of us have certain instincts when it comes to faith, and some of these instincts really are a little backwards, and in more than just one way. And for this reason, as much as we need it, faith fails to help us. This is what we are going to talk about tonight: understanding faith for what it really wants to be in our lives, so that it will give us what we need from it, and maybe much more than we ever expected.

"'Faith,'" said Father Mike. "We hear this word all the time, we use it ourselves, and yet so few of us really understand it.

"For most people in this world, 'faith' means something about the 'power of believing.'

"'If you really *believe* that something will happen,' they think, 'it will happen.' You have some kind of problem. You pray; you say to God, 'I really believe that You can do anything; I really believe that You are good and want to help me.' Then it's supposed to happen. If it doesn't happen, people sometimes blame themselves. 'I didn't *really* believe,' they say, by which they mean, 'I wasn't really *sure*.' Or they blame God and tell you, 'I don't know…I think I'm losing my faith.'"

Several people were nodding. In a couple of cases this meant that people agreed that this was not a good idea of faith; in the minds of other people it was wrong to give up on faith so fast.

"For many people," Father Mike continued, "faith is some vague sense that there is a greater power out there. We can get to Him. We can move Him with our pleading and our trust.

"When these people say that they believe 'in' things, like Jesus, or Mary, or the rosary, what they mean is: these are the words I use to call upon God, the words I use to do my pleading.

"Often when people are very fervent about their faith, their particular faith, what they really believe is that God has one particular formula for pleading that He wants us to use, and if we are loyal to it He will answer.

"Some people 'believe' the exact opposite. In their minds, all religions are really the same. 'It's the same God, isn't it, Father?' People like this idea because it means that it's all right to try praying in more than one kind of church, to try more than one way to plead. Maybe a combination will work!

"But none of this is what faith is really all about."

Here Father Mike paused. Then he said: "Faith is how we explain life. *Our* faith, the faith that supposedly we share, is our explanation of life in the light of our experience of God." He repeated this line slowly and emphatically. "Faith...is our *explanation* of life...in the light of our *experience* of God."

"Faith is how we understand why God made us, why we're here, why things happen we do not choose. This is what faith is really all about—how we explain life. This is what I propose to share with you tonight—the Church's explanation, from the ground up!"

At this, a variety of unseen emotions passed through the crowd. The most common one was hope.

THE BEGINNING OF FAITH

"So, how do we explain life?" began Father Mike. "Why are we here? Where do we come from?

"Let's start by noticing something fantastic. The question is the answer."

Father Mike continued: "The very fact that someone would ask this question, or understands it when someone else asks it, betrays a sense that everything comes from something greater. This, of course, is God. And seeing this, seeing the hand of God in the things He has made, is the beginning of faith.

"Actually," said Father Mike, "please permit me to talk about 'vision' instead of 'faith.' 'Faith,' as we have seen, conjures up in people's minds something about the 'power of believing' we can get what we want."

"What 'faith' really is is 'vision.' As it turns out, as we grow — which means becoming more and more developed in our minds and hearts — we see deeper and deeper into things, and what they are trying to tell us. More than learning specific facts about the world, we come to perceive something about the world in itself, about what reality *is*... that it comes from something much greater than us."

There was a moment of quiet and then Father Mike continued with a soothing voice.

"You can't do it now," he said, "but tonight, once you go to bed, before you fall asleep, and it is dark and quiet and there are no distractions, think about the simple fact that you are alive. Say to yourself 'I am' — not 'I am this or I am that' but simply 'I am' — and think about what you mean when you say it.

"Immediately you will realize that you are much more than you can possibly put into words. You can say certain things *about* you, but what you *are*, what you are being a person, is much too much to put into words.

"In this same moment, you will realize that you are much too much just to be here. You could not have come from nothing, for nothing, and be headed to nothing. You must have come from somewhere.

"This is human experience because, for all intents and purposes, creation was signed. Whenever you look closely at anything, you experience that it was made. This is God's signature on creation. Some say they can see it when they look at the majesty of the mountains. Others say they can see it when they look at the power of the sea. But you can even see the hand of God if you look at your own hand, not the fact that it works, but the very fact that it is there. You can see the hand of God best when you look at the thing you know best — yourself."

This idea was interesting to many people, but it produced more questions than clarity. One person decided to put his question into words. Surprising himself, James put up his hand.

"Please," said Father Mike, "questions are welcome."

"Excuse me, Father," said James, "maybe I know the feeling you're talking about, but it doesn't really *prove* anything, does it?"

"Thank you for asking this question," replied Father Mike. "You're bringing up something we *need* to talk about."

FAITH IS SCIENTIFIC

"Please understand," he said, "when we talk about 'proof,' we are using a word that doesn't really apply to the deep vision which is faith.

"But this doesn't mean that faith isn't scientific. In fact, faith is very scientific; let's think about it:

"Before a scientist can tell us anything that he has learned from his science, he has first perceived that what he learned studying the world *yesterday* will still be true *today*. His life in the world has told him that the world is dependable. This was the finding of no one experiment; it is what his whole life's experience has taught him — the world is dependable. He just knows it. He cannot prove it. There is nothing he can do today that will prove what must happen tomorrow, but the scientist is not worried. His whole life's experience has taught him — the world is dependable. He just knows it.

"Notice," said Father Mike, "no one is born with this idea, that the world is dependable."

Now James was nodding.

"Actually," continued Father Mike, "we are born with the idea that the world is *us*…that we *are* the world! A baby does not know that it is part of a larger world that is really 'out there.'

"And," said Father Mike with a slight change of tone, "when finally we figure this out, it bothers us that we still can't *prove* it. Haven't we all spent at least a couple of minutes wondering whether the whole world is just our dream — and then been a little frustrated to find out that there is nothing we can do to prove to ourselves it isn't?!"

Now several people were nodding.

"But we don't really doubt it. We just know it — that the world out there really exists. We are not born with this idea. It is the product of no one experience. We grow into it.

"And then," said Father Mike, "we grow into the idea that the world is dependable.

"But why should we presume that growth stops there?

"People of faith," said Father Mike, "experience even more about the world. *We* experience that the world is not only dependable but *dependent* — it must have come from somewhere.

"And why should "we NOT take seriously our experience of what reality is? Isn't going by your actual experience the whole idea of science?

"Well, our experience is that the world is not only dependable but dependent — it must have come from something greater. We can't really imagine that this *isn't* true.

"And we can't really imagine that the source of all things *isn't* as smart as we are, or *isn't* capable of feeling, or doesn't know that 'He' exists. So our experience actually tells us that the world must have come from some*one* greater.

"This is the vision which is faith. We perceive the deep truth about the world. We perceive God in the things He has made. And as we grow, we perceive Him more and more!

"For this reason, by the way, we do not need to be troubled by the question, Why can't we see God? As it turns out, we *do* see God, and, as we grow, we see God better and better, standing behind the things He has made.

"Are you still with me?"

Not everybody felt completely clear about the little speech they just heard, but nobody said "no" and so Father Mike continued.

HOW WE KNOW THAT WE WERE MADE FOR HEAVEN

"Okay, let's presume that we *do* see…we do perceive that God has made the world and us. So let's ask our-selves the next logical question, Why?

"Is it possible that God has made us just to live here and die and then be nothing?

"Why would He do that? Why would He give us life just to take it away? Why would He give us such a desperate desire to live…so that, really, we can barely imagine being nothing forever…if He was going to take life away?

"Isn't it clear…God made us for life, life with Him, life with Him forever? This is what we call heaven."

A couple of people were a little surprised. They hadn't heard the word "heaven" in quite some time.

This time it was Joy who spoke up. "I have a ques-tion," she said. "It sounds wonderful, but how do you know?"

"Another good question," responded Father Mike. "Let's look at it.

"Once again, tonight, once you go to bed, after you think about the fact that you are alive, take a few more seconds think about the idea of NOT being alive. Think about what death would seem to be. Like looking at the sun, you won't be able to do it long.

"Death would seem to be the end, the absolute end of *me* forever. If we can find the courage to face it for more than a few seconds, what we will feel is more terrible than we can possibly put into words. From deep within us a voice will cry out: 'No!' 'This cannot be!' 'There must be more to life than this!' This voice tells the truth.

"After all, made to want life so deeply as we do, if we were made for death, the God who made us would be cruel, something we cannot imagine God to be. Therefore, made to want life so deeply as we do, we know that we were made for life, eternal life."

Father Mike did not know that Joy had been struggling with thoughts of death for a while now. She listened to what he had to say with very mixed feelings. It sounded good; but it was disturbing to be asked to think about death *more*. She sat down, forced to think about it now, and Father Mike went on.

HOW TO IMAGINE HEAVEN

"And if you would like to have some idea of what heaven will be like, just look at what you were made to want. Now, I am *not* talking about the specific things you happen to want right now because this could change. No, I am talking about what all of us always want…the desires that come part and parcel with being alive."

"What do we want? We want *everything*. We want every good thing we see; we want to visit every interesting place we hear about, to have a great moment like every great moment we see someone else have, to be important to every interesting person out there.

"This is not so childish as maybe it seems. After all, we were made to share God's life, *divine* life. This is the source of every good thing we can experience here. This means that as we see good things here, we are learning more and more about what we are going to have in heaven. Of course, we want what we see.

"And we can use what we see to get an idea of heaven. Since divine life is going to be at least as good as anything we can have here, just imagine you had everything. Imagine the best life you possibly can—if anything were possible, FOR YOU. Admit to yourselves your wildest dreams—and I mean *wild*. I'm talking about the dreams you might have had as young people dreaming about fame, fortune, having someone you are crazy about fall in love with you...the dreams you would never admit to anyone else. Admit them to yourself and know that they are going to come true—*and more*, and so much more. This is what we mean by heaven."

At this a wide variety of thoughts were running through people's minds. Some were wondering whether they were hearing something wonderful—or too good to be true.

THE WORLD'S MOST IMPORTANT QUESTION THAT NEVER GETS ASKED

"Okay, once again I am going to presume I am making sense and you are with me. Let's move on to the next obvious question: if we were made to share God's life in heaven, why don't we have this life? What are we doing here on earth?"

"I'm sure you agree that this is a good question. After all, the best thing we believe would seem to be contradicted by the most obvious fact of the life we have."

This statement produced both agreement and a bit of surprise. "That's right," thought someone. "Why didn't I think about this before?" thought another.

"But this a question we can face," said Father Mike. "Let's begin with some things we know are true.

"We know that we come from something greater, and we know that greater also means smarter, wiser, doesn't do anything for nothing!

"This means we know that God put us here for a good reason—to give us something that even He could not just give us with the snap of His fingers.

"But what could this be? Well, what do we do here? Anyone?"

No hands went up, so Father Mike continued: "What we do is *grow*. We are born small and unformed, we don't know anything and we are self-centered, and we become more. *We* become more. And how we grow is much affected by *us*—what we do and what we don't do, what we choose, and how we try."

WHAT'S LOVE GOT TO DO WITH IT?

"And if we are really *growing*, becoming something *more*, we have more of what?"

People looked tentative. By now they were expecting Father Mike to answer his own question.

"*More* means growing in goodness, growing in love.

"Love is the greatest thing about us, is it not?"

At this point Henry had something to say. He raised his hand with a certain intensity, and Father Mike called on him immediately.

"Excuse me, Father, haven't the 'greatest' men of history been killers and dictators, and people who oppress everybody?"

Henry's question made people a little uncomfortable — but they knew it was a good question.

"You're right if 'great' means 'famous,'" replied Father Mike. "But I don't think it's true if we are talking about what we would expect to see if we could look inside a person. Great means 'more' and 'deeper' and 'bigger' in terms of heart. I don't think we experience greatness in a person with a little heart."

"But," added Father Mike, "I admit this wasn't always so. In the past, power, including the power to kill, looked great to many people. But as we as a people have grown, we see greatness in a deeper way."

Not unlike Joy, Henry felt more than a little conflicted. "I guess the answer makes sense," he thought, but thinking also of his recent struggles he also wondered, "isn't it greater to win?"

Father Mike accepted Henry's silence as permission to continue: "And as we are growing in love, aren't we becoming more and more like God — the God whose love, whose unselfishness, gave us life? And becoming more like God…shouldn't that allow us to understand Him better when finally He makes it possible for us to see Him? And won't this be our power to share His life more richly?

"This brings us to the real reason we are here before heaven?"

This focused people's attention.

"Because, through our own choices and our work, we are building the life we are going to have in heaven. God wants to involve us in our own creation. He is giving us the chance to be our own person, someone *we* made ourselves to be.

"And isn't this better than if He just made us without involving us?"

People thought this sounded right but weren't sure why.

Father Mike tried to explain it:

"When I talk about this with kids, I ask them, 'What do you appreciate better, a model plane you made yourself or something you just got out of a box?'

"When I talk about it with adults, I ask them, 'Which would you appreciate more—the life you built out of your own hard work, maybe overcoming many obstacles, or a life just won playing the lottery?'"

At that, people smiled.

"But there is even more we can say," said Father Mike. "The real reason we are here is something much deeper.

"God *doesn't* come from something greater. God just *is*. This is the essence of what it is to be God.

"Now, God can't give this to anyone—no, not even God can do that—make another God. Even God can't make a square circle."

Here Father Mike gave people a second to try to picture a square circle.

"But, by giving us a part in our own creation, God is letting us participate in the essence of divine life to the extent that a creature could."

Father Mike then repeated it with these words: "We are here to gain the creature's version of what it is to be like God.

"Please, let's make sure we get this…the practical meaning of what we are talking about: in the gaze of a loving God, the purpose of life is not staying out of hell; it is preparing to share God's life as richly as we might.

"Let's take a second to think about this, okay?"

Father Mike gave people not much more than a second.

AN INTRODUCTION TO THE IDEA OF GOD'S PLAN

"But, wait a second," he said, "if what we do to get ready for heaven is so important, why are we affected by so many things we do not choose? After all, nobody picks their parents, their birthday, or the century they're born into, or the country they're born into. And starting the very next day countless things we do NOT choose affect who we become, and they are happening right up to this very moment."

Again people nodded. Several were thinking of some not-so-nice things that had happened to them recently.

"So let's think it through together."

"When you and I do something—I like to use the example of throwing a ball against a wall—we have a pretty good idea of what will come from it. In the case of the ball, that's how we know where to go so we can catch it.

"But when God made the world—and, as far we know, this also involved throwing a ball—surely He knew exactly what would come from it. And exactly means exactly, everything, right down to the smallest detail.

"You and I could never keep track of something like this, but we *can* imagine it being done, and if we can imagine it, God must be able to do it. After all, our minds were invented by God; they cannot be capable of conceiving something greater than God.

Father Mike went on: "No, when you think about it, it is clear: when God made the world, He knew what was going to happen as this led to that, led to this, led to that, everywhere throughout the universe.

"He also knew that if He made it differently, it would have come out differently.

"So the world He *did* make contained His plan for everything that has ever happened and ever will.

"This means everything that led to you and me being conceived and born. This means what happened to us the next day, and the next day, and the next day, *knowing how we would react to things*.

"This is how God works with us, making us into the people He wants with Him in heaven…people He knows He can love with all His heart forever…AND, at the same time, letting us be the people that *we* made us to be!

WHY HARD THINGS HAPPEN

"Now, all of this might sound very reassuring at first hearing, but it also raises a question: after all, God's plan for *everything* is, well, God's plan for everything. But what about the hard, painful, even tragic things that happen to us? Why in the world would God plan things like that?"

Most people already had this question. They were eager for a good answer.

"Let's start by talking about the reason hard things are even *possible*. And to do this, we need to go back to the question: why are we *here*?

"We are here to participate in our own creation. We are here to grow. This means that we had to be made 'imperfect.' If we had been made 'perfect,' we would already be all that we can be—this is what 'perfect' means—and this means we could not grow. We would be done before we started. And imperfect doesn't mean that in some tiny ways we could make our mansion on the mountain nicer. No, if we are really here to put ourselves into the work of growing, it means there are things about us that we *really* don't want! It means that we start out with almost nothing, knowing nothing—

we call this 'ignorant' — and loving no one — we call this 'selfish' — and we never grow into something nearly as great as we want. It means that we will make some mistakes that will really cause trouble. It means we can be hurt — and when we *are* hurt, it *does* hurt.

Many people now thought of some particular time they had been hurt. Gloria was feeling hurt anew.

"But there is more that we say," continued Father Mike. "Let me point out that if we never experienced anything as really bad, we wouldn't really experience anything as really good either. Part of what makes things good is knowing that it doesn't have to be; it is something that could be much *less* than what we have; it represents something *bad* that we have conquered, or avoided.

"Also, if nothing were experienced as bad, we would have no real reason to work for anything — to go in one direction instead of another.

"And, like nothing else, suffering makes us give ourselves to the work of life? Nothing makes us dig so deep, to who we really are, to find out what we really believe, in order to go on. Like nothing else, dealing with things that can cause suffering make us make…us."

At this point Gloria spoke up. "Really, Father, is what we go through really worth it? I mean, the price some people pay…what did you say…to make us make us?"

Father Mike responded, cautiously. "Speaking for myself," he said, "I have been through some hard things.

Some were really hard at the time. I was tempted to cry; maybe I did. And then time went by and I saw what came from it. Maybe it was something new and deeper in me. Maybe it was an opportunity I would never have had otherwise. A new person in my life. And now I say, 'I'm happy I went through it.'"

Various people thought of similar situations in their own lives, but Gloria was not yet able to do the same.

"But," Father Mike continued, in a lower and humbler tone, "I know there is terrible suffering in the world, and I am not trying to say explanations can take it away. But understanding does make things less terrible, and the more we understand, the better. Even in our worst moments, it leaves us with the hope that someday we will be happy again, and even happy that we went through the hardest things we had to go through. It can help us to look forward through the pain to the wonderful, glorious things that God is bringing about through it.

"And we can be sure of this: God in His goodness would not have asked us to go through difficult things if it were not to give us SO MUCH more than He could have given us without them."

HOW WE GO TO HEAVEN

"You see," said Father Mike, "the value of everything we go through here, and every little bit we grow, is VASTLY magnified once our work on earth is over.

"Please let me clarify this," he said. "We are here, not to become the people that we are going to be in heaven, we are here to become the seeds of the people we are going to be in heaven. We are here to become the *seeds* we will be at the end of our lives, seeds that God will then transform and bring to the full life of heaven.

"You know how seeds work. Seeds are little tiny things that don't look like much; but we bury them in the ground; they disintegrate; and out of their integration comes something so much bigger and more beautiful than the seed that it came from—so much more than this seed could ever have imagined.

"And you also know this about seeds: you cut one open and what do you see? You *don't* see a little flower. You don't see a little tree. What you see makes no sense—until it grows. Then we see how this became a branch or how something else became a leaf. It's the same way with a lot that we have inside us, things that we've been through. Right now it's not clear why we struggled with this, why we went through that. But once our work on earth is finished, and God transforms us, we will see what wonderful things have come from what we went through.

"Any questions about this?"

It was James who again surprised himself by speaking up. "Okay, so *how* is God supposed to transform us? And into what?"

Father Mike nodded slowly. "Excellent question. I hope you will feel you are getting a good answer. God will transform us by remaking us in spirit—the stuff of God Himself—so now we can see Him."

James knew that this was not an adequate answer.

Father Mike knew he needed to say more: "Right now," he said, "what *are* we? People might want to say that 'we are our soul.''' Several people nodded.

"But what is a soul?" Not waiting for anyone to answer, Father Mike promptly offered this: "Our soul is the 'who' that arises from the network of our memories."

Some people started to feel a little frustrated.

Father Mike knew he needed to continue quickly: "You know you are a 'who.' It's the thing you think of when we say 'you.'

"And 'you' are different from someone else most obviously because of what? You are you and not that person over there because you have a lifetime of different memories.

"Now, right now, here on earth, our memories of are made of matter. You know where your memories are"—Father Mike tapped his head—"and you know what this thing is made of. But we can imagine memories being made of something else. And the 'something else' we know about is spirit—the stuff of God Himself.

"And what, exactly, is that? Well," said Father Mike, "we know what matter is—more or less. Spirit is something greater—the stuff that made matter.

"And once we are remade, out of the stuff of God Himself, we will be able to see Him.

"And seeing Him face to face will teach us more in a moment than we could have learned in a billion years here on earth, where we see God only partly, and learn about Him bit by bit.

"Seeing God face to face will, in a moment, make us all we can be. This is how we 'go to heaven.'

The phrase "face to face" got some people to picture an old man; it got others to picture a bright light.

Father Mike continued: "See how wise it was of God to make us as He did! He gets us to be the people that *He* wants us to be—people He wants to spend eternity with, people He knows He can love with all His heart forever—and at the same time we do the work of reacting, of thinking, of trying, failing, learning, and growing, and making ourselves the people that we want us to be."

"Any more questions?" he asked.

QUESTIONS AND ANSWERS

Several hands went up. Father Mike called on the person who seemed the most intent; it was Mark. "So we're not really free, then? I mean we think we're free but it's really God pulling the strings."

"Very fair question," said Father Mike, "and the only way I can respond to it is to ask you to put up with a little study of what 'freedom' is really all about.

"Let's start by saying that freedom is *not* some power to make choices that even God did not see coming. It does not mean that a person can make choices apart from his past experience. Freedom means that our choices come from *us*; they are not forced from the outside or otherwise compelled by something that we, as the persons *we are*, did not choose."

Here Father Mike addressed Mark directly. "Am I making sense, so far?" he asked.

"Yes," replied Mark, volunteering nothing more.

"Okay," said Father Mike, continuing to speak to Mark. "And so, these choices that reflect us…how do they affect us?"

"They change us," said Mark, halfway between an answer and a question.

"Yes," reacted Father Mike with a mixture of enthusiasm and gratitude. "So, a little more than yesterday, the person who faces what will come into our lives tomorrow is the product *of* us. A lifetime of this process is personal responsibility; it realizes the purpose of our life here before heaven. BUT our choices are still based on what we know and feel; they are based on what we have experienced in our lives. The fact that God has planned our lives so that we will, in the end, make ourselves into people He knows He can love…well, that was just plain smart."

At this point, Mary raised her hand and asked: "So this applies to everyone?" Father Mike nodded.

"It doesn't seem fair" was Mary's reaction. "I mean, God gives to some people a lot more opportunity to grow than others. And what about babies who die, or are miscarried or…. How is this God's plan?"

Everyone knew that this was a good question.

"That is a really good question," acknowledged Father Mike, "and I hope you will find that the answer is breathtaking!"

Many people shifted in their seats.

WE WERE MADE TO BE A FAMILY

"This is a really big idea," said Father Mike, "and when you include it with everything else we have already seen, it makes sense of *everything*....

"We are here, not merely to become the individuals we are going to be in heaven, but rather the *family* that we are going to be.

"Again," he said, "let us think this through together.

"God, we can say, is a like a family. God is more than one person as you and I are one person.

"What I mean by this is this: did you ever think about the fact that so many things that God has made, for example, friendship, romance, *baseball*...are things that would never have existed if God had made only one person?"

A couple of people tried quickly to picture themselves alone in the universe. It was not easy.

Father Mike went on: "This means that these things, in some form, must have existed *in* God already. Even God cannot give what He does not have.

"God is more than a person. He is more than what one person can know by him or herself.

"This is the reason He made a family with whom to share His life.

"And we are going to share God's life *as* a family, sharing with each other what each one sees in God, just like in a family, the way families are supposed to be! This way, in the end, all of us will share fully in what our family gets from God. And this is right because each of us has had a role in the making of our family, the role that God gave us.

"Okay," said Mary, without raising her hand. "But how does any of this help a person who died as a little baby."

"Another really good question," said Father Mike, "Let's see if we can get to an answer together.

"In order to make it right that we share God's life as a family, God is making us through the work of each other.

"This is the reason God has made us by means of human history where what *we* have is owed to people of times past who did not have the same advantages that we have to know and to grow.

"Think about it. We are able to be together tonight, and talk about some really important things using *language*. But we did not invent language. Language was invented through the struggles of centuries of people that might not have been very *holy* as we normally think of 'holy' today. But their job was to give us language so that our family, their family, could go forward.

"Think about this too. If the purpose of history is to make us grow, this means that, over time, more and more people will do better and better. But this also means that at any one time many people will be behind those who were given by God to lead the way! If you and I have been given more than many, I think it's for us to feel grateful, and to be reminded that our human family still has a long way to go.

"And now, thanks to the idea we were made to be family, maybe we can make sense of the death of a baby. It is true that the baby didn't grow much, but his birth and his loss affects history; it affects the parents, and their friends, and lots of other people the baby did *not* grow up with. These effects are painful at first—very painful—but in the end they will lead us to becoming precisely the family that God wants with Him in heaven, a family perfectly prepared, according to His plan, to share His life as richly as any family ever could.

"The people of times past, troublesome people of today, every single baby…they all have their part to play in making us the family that we were meant to be, and they all belong at the table, at the banquet of heaven.

"Actually," said Father Mike, "the idea of a banquet is one of our best images of how heaven will work. Imagine a banquet," he said, "being shared by a group of people who love one another. It's easy to imagine that each one has brought a dish—not the same dish, not the same size, but in every case something good—and now everyone is welcome to share in all there is.

"This does not seem fair," interjected Henry with a tone that almost indicated anger. "After all, why should I try real hard to do the right thing when this other guy does everything wrong and he's going to be in the same place as me?"

Once again one person had done a good job of speaking for almost all.

"Let's start by thinking of this," replied Father Mike. "It is love that will give us a greater life with God. But how is what I am doing really love if I am doing it for my reward only?!

"No, it's really love when I am doing it for more than just me. It's really love when I am doing it for people I will *love* personally when I see them in heaven…people I will appreciate for who God made them to be, and for the part in His plan that He needed them to play."

This sounded right to most, but to others it sounded like something was missing. So quickly for them, Father Mike added another point: "And if you think this means you can just sit back and do just as well as you can by doing nothing, please think of this: for every bit you grow, and help others to do the same, all of us, INCLUDING YOU, will have a richer life with God forever!"

Mark was again involved: "So," he said, "no matter what happens we just say, 'I guess that was God's plan' and everything is fine. Then what difference does it make what we do?"

"Well," responded Father Mike, "faith in God's plan does NOT mean that it does not matter what we do. God's plan *will* guarantee that we become the family best prepared to share His life, but how good is our family's best?! This is still in the process of being decided, by you and me!

"It is true that once things have happened and cannot be changed, we say that God's plan has spoken. But what about the future? From our point of view, this is not decided; and we can affect it, for better or for worse. Actually, we have no choice but to affect it; even to do nothing is itself a decision! Our job, then, is to do our best as we see it, with peace that God will work with whatever comes out, and with the excitement of knowing that we can make 'forever' better.

"This, then, is the great purpose of life — to grow in faith and love and help others do the same so that our family will have a richer life with God forever."

Henry again spoke up: "So we will see Hitler in heaven?"

People were quite interested in what Father Mike might say.

"Before I answer that let me throw out this question," he said. "Does anyone's idea of God really go together with the idea that someone is going to be tortured in hell forever?"

Not waiting for a response, Father Mike continued: "I think we need to be careful about judging people and declaring who is 'really' bad, really bad compared to me!

"But," continued Father Mike, "I know that in some cases it's hard *not* to judge. The struggle of human history has been just that — a struggle! — and working our way out of pure selfishness with no conscience has produced some people who have done some very horrible things. AND," said Father Mike forcefully, "it would be wrong to say that God 'wanted' these things as though He enjoyed watching or wants them to keep on happening, BUT:

"To grow into what is good, we had to grow out of what is *not* good, we had to grow out of what is bad; and to grow into to what is great, we had to grow out of what is very bad.

"And because God is good we can also count on this," added Father Mike: "Out of everything awful God has asked us to conquer, He is actually giving us something glorious that we could not have gotten otherwise.

"As for those who represent the worst in us"—here there was a pause—"when we think of them let us think of this:

"Sometimes the hard work of life is experienced *here*, when we suffer, and especially when we suffer because of the bad acts of others, and sometimes the hard work of becoming God's family is experienced *there*, when we have to face the truth of what is good and bad, and reconcile ourselves with anyone we might have hurt, BUT:

"Once we are transformed by God so that we can see Him, and see with perfect clarity the truth of what is good and bad and everything else, our sorrow will be utterly sincere and deep, and our power to express our sorrow will be as great as it could be.

"And the love of others will be great, too, and with it their power to forgive.

"Let us also remember," continued Father Mike, "that we are already called to love as our work on earth, and this already means compassion. And we are called to grow in love; and this means more and more compassion. And if it sometimes seems that we are being asked for 'too much'…well, isn't struggle for more the way we grow? Shouldn't we feel called to the greatest love we can conceive?"

This line provoked reflection but Father Mike didn't give people much time.

"Besides," he added, "if others are evil because of their selfish or even 'sick' choices, what should I think about me — considering all I have been given to help me do better? Whereas, if I can affirm the goodness deep within others, all others, then, maybe, I can believe in the goodness deep within me.

"Does anyone need a break?" he now asked.

"Yes!" said Irene as she made a rush for the rest-room.

FAITH AS THE RIGHT REASON TO BELIEVE IN YOURSELF

Father Mike did not give people much of a break; and he began again right where he left off: "Okay," he said, "speaking of believing in ourselves…. I would like us to take a look at this: Not only does the idea that 'we were made to be a family' help us to make sense of the idea of God's plan, it can help us to understand ourselves as individuals.

"But shouldn't we have expected this?" asked Father Mike, though this was not a question. "After all, if we *were* made to be a family, how could we expect to understand ourselves apart from this idea?" Also not a question.

It wasn't a question, but some of the people did ponder it.

"Again," asked Father Mike, "please think this through with me.

"The purpose of God's plan is that we become the family best prepared to share God's life forever, with each person having his or her part to play in the making of this family, and each person having his or her place in heaven, seeing God in his or her own way, with this to share with everyone else.

"Now," said Father Mike, "God is infinite, not limited in any way. We can say this because…well, how could there be something 'more' that God does not have? Where would 'more' come from?!"

"How could there be something 'more' that God does not have?" A couple of people wished that Father Mike had given them more time to think about this.

Instead he continued: "This means that God is capable of putting infinite attention into every detail of absolutely everything He does. And we know He does this because He would have NO reason not to.

"*This* means that God has put all He has into His plan for each of His children, and this means that He has put all He has into His plan for you, AND NO LESS than He has put into His plan for anyone else, not anyone.

"This is how each of us is absolutely 'special,' which actually means 'carefully made and good in your own way,' and no less than anyone else!

"This is the right reason for each of us to be thrilled to be who we are, and to have the special struggle which is our life. Through this struggle God is making you the absolutely special person that you will be in heaven, who is being prepared to see Him as no one else will, and who will get from this sight what all of us will need.

"And this means that you will have a beauty and importance far, far greater than anything that anyone has here!"

People never expected that they would be hearing such a thing, ever. Once again, some wondered whether it might not be too good to be true.

Father Mike continued: "You see what you get from faith—to love yourself for the right reason, because God has made you who you are.

"*This* is the right reason to love yourself. It has to do with who you are in the eyes of your Maker. It has to do with who the rest of us will see when our work on earth is finished.

"It does not involve something that can change, something you can lose like popularity, power, or the love of another human person—who is still a *human* person who is always struggling with selfishness and may not always love you well.

"Best of all, if you love yourself for the right reason, because God has made you who you are, and you know that He has put no less into you than He has put into anyone else, you are freed to see the goodness of everyone else.

"If you think about this," said Father Mike, "you will see that it is true: If you believe that you are no less special than anyone else, you have no need to think that you are more special.

"This is how God made us — so that all of us could be completely happy to be who we are.

"And, again," continued Father Mike, "if you love yourself, you are freed to love others.

"It's a 'saying' in faith: if you love yourself, you will always love others. If you love yourself, you feel good and, automatically, you want to do good — you want to love. This is how our goodness is us being like God.

"But if you do not love yourself, you cannot love others. What, after all, is love? Love is when you see the goodness beyond yourself. But if you don't see the goodness within yourself, the goodness out there will bother you. It will make you feel 'less.'

"Whereas, if you do see the goodness within you — because you know the truth, regardless of how other people might have treated you — the goodness out there doesn't bother you at all. You are free to see the goodness God put in others and to love, and there again is the eternal purpose of life!

"But there is more! Love of self is what we call a 'gift' of faith."

THE GIFTS OF FAITH

"The 'gifts' of faith are the effects on our spirit that follow, automatically, when we see things in the light of what faith tells us.

"For example," said Father Mike, "how would you feel if you knew that you were going to get $100 million for next Christmas?"

As always, people laughed at this line. Many people knew right away what they would do with *some* of the money.

"How would you feel if you knew that you were going to get $100 million for next Christmas?" Father Mike repeated the question. Then he answered it: "You would be happy *now* — before you got a single cent! Just knowing it was coming, you would be overjoyed.

"And your joy wouldn't last just a day. You would think about it every day; you would dream about how it was going to be; and this would be the greatest joy of all.

"What you didn't have right now wouldn't mean a thing! Indeed, what you didn't have right now would only inspire you to dream.

"Well," said Father Mike, "heaven *is* coming. And it's better than $100 million.

"You might have to wait more than a year or two to get there. But when finally your time has come, heaven is forever.

"You see," said Father Mike, "just knowing something would change completely how you feel about everything!

"This is what I mean by a gift of faith.

"Let's go through them.

"Let's start with what we get for faith in God's plan.

"Faith in God's plan lets us love ourselves for the right reason, because we see that right now, so far, we are exactly who God has made us be.

"This means no more comparing ourselves to others. No more criticizing ourselves for what we cannot yet do or have done and cannot change.

"Comparing ourselves to others and criticizing ourselves for something we cannot change, that's how we torture ourselves, isn't it?"

People nodded.

Father Mike continued: "Faith in God's plan allows us to accept whatever has happened and cannot be changed. We may *not yet* know why something hard has happened, but we can know *that* it needed to happen, for the best possible reason. We can know that *when* we see what came from it, we'll be happy, really happy, we went through it.

"My guess is that you know people," said Father Mike, "who have been carrying on about something that happened, maybe *twenty* years ago."

People smiled. Henry thought about himself.

"They are tormented *because* whatever happened can't be changed. But for us, with the vision which is faith…once we see that something can't be changed… that's when the peace begins!"

More smiling—except from Henry.

Father Mike continued: "Since we know that everything that is going to happen—once it has happened and cannot be changed—will also follow God's plan, we can live our lives without fear.

"After all, if we know that a year from now we are going to be exactly where God wants us to be, what is there to fear?

"If we think the same thing about our family and friends, we can live without the impossible burden of thinking that everything depends on us. Everything does not depend on us. Everything depends on God. Our job is to do our best, the best we can right now. The rest is up to God and His plan.

"Now," said Father Mike, "let's look at the gifts that follow from faith in love.

"Faith in love inspires us to do *our* part. We know why we are here. We know what we should do. We know that what we do will make an eternal difference.

"After all," clarified Father Mike, "if we believe that we are here to grow in love, we love. We are free—free from the 'fear' that we are doing more than others—to live the only kind of life that could ever satisfy us.

"God is no fool." This was a little jarring. "He would not have made us so that we could ever be happy going the wrong way. Rather, He made us so that we can be happy only when we are going the right way. This is the reason that if we live selfishly we are never satisfied, no matter how much we have, whereas if we live a life of love we are always satisfied, no matter how little we have."

"Excuse me," said Gloria even though she had the feeling that she was interrupting.

"Please," said Father Mike.

"'No matter how little'...is that really true?"

"Fair question," responded Father Mike. "Maybe I'm trying to say too much too fast." A couple of people already thought this. "But I'm NOT trying to say that things that cost money, and other facts of life that affect our lifestyle are not at all important. I know they *do* help us to be happy — and they come from God and they help us imagine life with God. But, alone, they cannot make us happy. With faith, on the other hand, there is always a core of peace within us; and this peace makes it possible for us to anticipate the place where we're going… the place where we're going to have everything, forever. In this way, I think, the most satisfying feelings a person can have can still be ours. And yours."

Gloria appreciated that last line.

"And now let's think of this," continued Father Mike, "if to grow in faith and love is our goal, we get a gift that no one expects — control! We are always in a position to do what we want most of all."

"How can this be?" thought a couple of people quickly.

"We do not have control if fame or fortune is our goal," explained Father Mike. "If something worldly is our goal, we have to hope that the world will cooperate. Probably it will not! If, instead, to grow in faith and love is our goal, we can always do what we want, no matter what. Nothing can stop us. If something goes wrong, we can accept it, and our faith will still grow. If people offend or disappoint us, we can forgive them, and our love will still grow."

"Now," said Father Mike, "let's talk about the gifts that follow from faith in heaven.

"From faith in heaven we get the most of all:

"Faith in heaven frees us from the dread of death, or the need to run around and keep ourselves distracted—never really living—because we cannot face the facts of life.

"Faith in heaven frees us from anguish at the death of those we love. Though we may miss them, we know that they have gone to God and are more alive than we are. We also know that, soon enough, we will be reunited."

Joy reacted to that.

"And knowing we're not going to lose them, we feel freer to love them while they're here."

Mary reacted to this one.

"Faith in heaven lets us dream."

"We already talked about this," said Father Mike, "everybody grows up with dreams. But then the dreams die; and people try to put them out of their heads; but they never really do completely. What is worse, at least on television, they constantly see people who seem to have it all. The result of all this is that, deep-down, their own lives end up in disappointment." Now there was another pause. "This never happens to people of faith. We know that our dreams are going to come true, the only place they ever could.

"What is more, knowing that we were made for life with God, divine life, we understand that we were made to want divine life. We understand that no worldly thing will ever satisfy us completely. This is the reason that to get one thing is to want another, and then another; and to fix one problem is to get another, and then another.

"With faith in heaven we know better than to say those awful words 'if only.' 'If only this, I would be happy. If only not that, everything would be alright.' We know that everything would be alright for about two minutes — maybe a couple of days — and then it would be 'if only' something else.

"No, with faith in heaven we do not suffer what we do not have.

"We do not suffer envy.

"And, *not* seeking more from things than they can give, we can enjoy the things we do have. Our house does not have to be a heavenly mansion. Our house is not in heaven. But, if we find love there, it can still be a home. The people in our lives do not need to be perfect. You're not perfect! But, if people are trying, they can still be our companions."

COUNTING THE GIFTS OF FAITH

"Look at what faith wants to give you...."

Father Mike now held up his right index finger.

"*Love* of self. Because we realize that God has made us who we are."

Two fingers. (You get the idea.)

"*Peace* with what we cannot change. Because we realize that whatever cannot be changed happened for God's good reasons.

"Freedom from fear and pressure. Because we know that everything that is going to happen will also follow God's plan.

"Freedom to *love* and therefore to live the only life that can bring us happiness. Because we know that love is what life is for — and it doesn't matter whether we are rewarded here.

"*Control*. Because we can always do what we want most.

"Freedom from the *dread* of death — or the need to live a life distracted. Because we know that death is not the end.

"Freedom from *anguish* at the death of those we love. Because we know that they are alive with God and that someday we are going to be reunited.

"Freedom to *dream* joyfully. Because we know that the greatest life we can imagine, and more, is on the way.

"Freedom from longing and *envy*. Because we know we were made for life with God and nothing here can fill us.

"The ability to *enjoy* what we already have. Because we do not expect things to be more than they can be."

There was a gift of faith for each finger.

"All this," declared Father Mike, "for seeing the plain truth of the basics we have looked at tonight.

"And, just in case you were wondering...."

Actually, at this point, most people were a little tired.

WHERE JESUS AND THE CHURCH FIT IN

"Because we are going to share God's life as a family, obviously we are 'in this together' here.

"For this reason God made us with a built-in motive to get together and to work together.

"This is reason our lives are always richer when we share them; and our faith is stronger when we share it.

"That's why God wants us to be a family of faith here on earth.

"But if God wanted us to be a family, He had to send someone to call us to be a family. A family in faith cannot come together by some grand coincidence of agreement. This is where Jesus comes into the picture. At another time we might want to talk about this.

"We might also want to talk about how Jesus' cross proclaimed the basics we have talked about tonight. But quickly…. If someone gives up his life and *lives*, don't you see heaven? If someone gives up his life and gets to glory, don't you see the glory in love? If someone gives up his life because God the Father doesn't give him a better option not to, and *it works out*, don't you see the wisdom of God's plan?

"And don't you see that it was really at the last supper where Jesus gave up his life in the sense that it was there that he committed himself not to run and to risk the cross…and this gave us something we could repeat where we can see Jesus giving up his life; and it blesses something we can *receive personally* that communicates the love that was proclaimed on the cross;and it established the meal, our Mass, that makes us a family in faith?

"And we might also notice that the rest of Jesus' life, and all he had to go through, was planned to inspire all of God's sons and daughters no matter what we might have to go through according to His plan."

Now people were even more tired!

"But let's leave all this for another time," said Father Mike. "Maybe Father Ed will invite me back."

FIVE WAYS WE GET FAITH BACKWARDS

"For now let me finish by explaining the title of this talk just in case you didn't already see it. I hope you have noticed that we have talked about several ways that people get faith backwards."

Once again with fingers!

"First, I hope I was clear: Faith is not about believing in what we cannot see; faith is about seeing!

"Life is not about staying out of hell; life is about gaining the richest life that can God give us.

"Life is not about *me* getting to heaven; it is about *us* getting ready for heaven.

"God loves you for who He made you. God does not love you despite you. And He loves you no less than He loves anyone else.

"One more. One more way we get faith backwards. It is the idea we started with, the idea that faith means that if I really believe something will happen, it will happen. This is not faith. Faith is really believing in God, that God is God, and He knows better than I do what I need so I will be ready for the life that lasts forever.

"Now, I am not saying that it is wrong to pray for things. To have a relationship with anyone we need to tell this person how we feel. The same is true of our relationship with God. And when we do speak to Him out of our hearts we will feel heard, and we will know that He is there, and He is God, and He has our lives securely in His hands. That's why we pray for what we think we need, and then we say 'but Thy will be done.' Thy will be done; You know better than I do what I need and I know the best thing will happen. *This* faith is sure to give you the best thing in life which is peace.

"The best thing in life *is* peace; and I hope I have encouraged yours a little bit tonight. Thank you for coming."

Father Mike got a generous applause. In the meeting and greeting that followed several people asked, "Would it be okay if I called you, to talk about some things?" "Of course," he said. In the days ahead a couple of these people called, and a couple of others as well. These included Gloria and Joy who left knowing they were going to call, and Mark and Henry who did not. ∎

PART III:
FAITH SPEAKS TO

◉

MARK

Mark did not know he was going to call. Not the same night as Father Mike's talk. But something stayed with him. It wasn't something very specific. It was more of an impression, the impression that there was a way to look at life that was a lot brighter than his. It was out of character and a little scary to ask for an appointment with a "father"; but, in the end, Mark decided he was going nowhere on the road he was on and so, why not "take a shot"?

Father Mike's appointment room was comfortable. There was no desk, just a couple of chairs, a little table, and something that held files. The artwork on the walls was unusual but didn't get Mark's attention.

"I really don't know where to start," he said.

"Start anywhere," said Father Mike, "and if you say something I don't understand, I'll ask."

Mark started his story. He did not start with anything about his childhood or adolescence. It would never have occurred to him to talk about such things.

"I just can't get a break," he said.

"What do you mean?"

"You work hard. You do things right. You are supposed to get ahead. But it just doesn't happen. Instead, you get screwed. People take advantage of you. And you can't give your family the things you want to give them."

"What kind of work do you do?"

"I'm in distributing."

"Distributing what?"

"Plumbing supplies."

"For stores, builders, who?"

"Mostly contractors — who don't pay until they feel like it."

Father Mike smiled. "Have you been in the business a long time?" he asked.

"Twelve, fifteen years," said Mark.

"How has the business changed?"

"What do you mean?"

"I am thinking that fifteen years is a long time in the trades. Things seem to change all the time."

"Materials," said Mark, slightly struck by this turn in the conversation. "It used to be all metal and now it's almost all plastic."

"Does that make it cheaper to keep inventory?"

"No," said Mark, "the opposite. These plastics are supposed to last forever. They're expensive."

"How many different products do you need to carry?"

"A lot."

The conversation continued along these lines for a while. Mark began to lighten up, a little pleased at feeling "interesting." He *did* know his business, and he had learned the hard way, on his own. And he was a little proud that he also knew why American plumbing is less fussy than the systems in other countries, and the answer to all the other questions that Father

Mike asked him. He was almost disappointed when Father Mike apologized for asking so many questions and now asked "what brought you in to talk to me today?"

Mark was less angry than when he came in, but he remembered that he wanted to talk about anger.

"So," said Father Mike, "you believe you are angry because life is not treating you fairly?"

"It *isn't*," replied Mark.

"Would you say that life treats most people fairly?"

Mark had to think about this for a second. Finally, he said, "No." Even as he said it he wondered whether it should make him feel worse, or better.

"So, maybe," said Father Mike, "the problem is with life."

"What do you mean?"

"You said you came to my talk last week."

"Yes."

"Do you remember that we talked about life with God, and I said that because we were made for life for life with God, we were made to *want* this life, and for this reason there will always be a huge distance between what we want and what we have here? This is the reason that nothing here can ever fill us. You get this, you want that, you get that, you want something else. You fix this problem, you get another, you fix that problem, something else happens."

"I do remember that," said Mark, and this very thought had struck him as something-worth-remembering the first time he heard it.

Father Mike went on: "This, I think, is the main reason there is so much anger in the world—because of the big distance there is between what people want and what they can have."

Now into Mark's mind popped the picture of a much bigger house. He started to imagine a much sexier…. Father Mike kept talking:

"The problem is that people don't realize that this is always true for everyone *here on earth*. They don't realize that the happiness we *can* have comes from understanding this, and from *not* expecting life here to be what it cannot be, and from accepting that the struggle to deal with this is the way we get ready for the life where we *will* have everything that we were made to want.

"Now," continued Father Mike, "I'm not saying it's bad to want good things. And, certainly, there are certain basic things we need. But what, really, do we *need*?"

"Is it wrong to enjoy life?" Mark knew that this was a good question—and he also knew that the answer had to be "no."

"No," said Father Mike. "I'm NOT saying it's wrong to enjoy life. But, enjoying life, having *joy*, has to do with living well, and doing with life what life is for!

"That's why the happiest people you'll ever meet are rarely rich; they are people who have figured out that they come from God and are here on earth to get ready for life with God forever; and they're working on it.

"The way God made us…we were made so that we would have a built-in motive to go the right way. That's why when we are working on growing in our faith and love we always feel good—we feel that we are growing into a greater life—and when we are living for this world where we really have NO future, we don't feel good.

"Is this making sense?"

"Maybe," said Mark, "or maybe it's an excuse for not being successful."

"Maybe," said Father Mike, "but what, really, is success? What's the success that lasts…that doesn't get wiped out with time?"

"Think about it," asked Father Mike, "if we were made for life with God, and life here is about helping God to give us more, how could we possibly live well not knowing this?"

This was not a question.

"We see it all the time, don't we," asked Father Mike, "people who seem to have everything—they are rich, they are famous, they have a beautiful wife—and then they wreck their lives doing something stupid because all they had just wasn't enough?"

Mark did see this "all the time." "What's wrong with these people?" he said.

"Nothing's really wrong with them," replied Father Mike. "Actually, I would say that something is right with them. They are NOT experiencing worldly things as enough to make them happy."

Father Mike now added this: "Besides, what would it say about God if He made the world, and us, so that only the rich and famous could be happy?

"Think about it, Mark. Fame and fortune are necessarily limited. If everybody's famous, nobody's famous; if everybody's rich, nobody's rich. Does it really make sense that God would make the world so that real happiness is available only to a few even though He made us so that everybody wants it?

"Is being rich and famous really what everybody wants?" Now it was Mark's turn to ask a question that was not really a question.

"It's not what most people will admit," said Father Mike, answering anyway. "But, deep down, it's what many, many people feel. It's one of the things that makes for the big distance between what they have and what they want; or maybe I should say the big distance between what they want to be and what they *are*."

"What do you mean?"

"In today's world, people grow up seeing a lot— mostly on television. And, of course, a lot of what they see looks good; and if they see it, and it looks good, they want it. This includes a lot of things most people won't admit to wanting, at least not when they get older, like being some really powerful person who gets attention all the time, being cheered for in some stadium, being so rich that if you can think it you can have it."

Mark said nothing but he was thinking. He remembered his dreams of hearing the cheering in some stadium. At least to himself he was willing to admit it.

Father Mike went on: "Then real life comes along and we kind of figure out that it's not going to happen. But we still watch TV and we see *other people* who seem to have it. And when this happens it's hard not to feel envy. Am I still making sense?"

"I guess so," said Mark. In fact, he knew that it was true; and he felt a little embarrassed. But then he thought, "If we can talk about this out loud, how terrible can it be?"

"Envy is a big source of anger," continued Father Mike, "but what makes things even worse is the feeling, 'they did it, why couldn't I do it?' Now we feel like some kind of failure."

Mark didn't like hearing the word "failure," not one bit, but he had come to talk about serious things and so he decided to continue listening. That didn't seem like something that a failure would do.

"Let me throw a thought at you," said Father Mike with a slight change of tone that suggested he was slightly changing the subject. "Most of the time, when people are often angry, they are mostly angry at themselves. People who are happy with themselves are happy, and even though they still have problems and sometimes get annoyed, they wouldn't describe themselves as 'angry.' Does this make sense?"

"You think I'm angry with myself?"

"What I think, Mark," replied Father Mike, "is that in today's media-driven world, where most people spend so much time watching and talking about a few, most people have been given the idea that they are really 'nobody.' And this, I think, would make anybody angry."

Just hearing this started to make Mark angry.

"The real tragedy," continued Father Mike, "is that the exact opposite is true."

Mark had no idea about what this might mean, but he hoped that it was true.

Father Mike continued: "You heard me say this last week:

"Each of us was made by God to play a part in His plan for the world that no one else can play, and to prepare to have a place in the family we will be in heaven that no one else can fill.

"Each of our lives was planned by God with infinite care, and this means NO LESS than anyone else, so that we can become the absolutely special and hugely important person we will be."

Mark did remember this. At the time he remembered imagining that he was the center of attention in some big place filled with people.

Father Mike kept talking: "The only question is *how* important? How well are we going to be able to understand God when finally we see Him face to face, so that we will have more to share with everyone else? How much are we going to grow, to become more like

God, before we go to see Him? This question is still to be decided — by us! And the process starts when we realize that we are already very, very big deals in the eyes of our Creator. Only then — when we realize that we already are what we so deeply want to be — can we afford to see the beauty in others, and to love them, and to grow, and to get more to bring to the table of heaven."

"Actually," said Mark, "I have a question." Actually, Mark had this question from the first time he had heard about how "special" everybody is.

"Please."

"It sounds good, for sure. That there's a really good reason for everything that a person has gone through in his life. That everybody is special and — how do you keep saying it? — NO LESS than anyone else. But how does believing that we are 'no less special than anyone else' make it true? It doesn't look true. It doesn't look like everyone is so great.

"Well, Mark, when *I* look, what I see is that God is God, and God is infinite, and He was able to put all He has into the making of each one of us. And certainly He made us so that we *want* to be no less special than anyone else!

"And, if you want to see some of the greatness that God is building into you, then DO believe in you. Stop comparing yourself to others and try to think about how thrilled you should be that God has made you who you are so far.

"And don't think that doing this is too easy to mean anything! Doing this is NOT easy. After all, to love yourself is to accept your limitations. It is to accept the things about yourself that you would like to change but can't. It is to accept that, right now, you have less than others.

"This takes a lot of faith, a lot of faith in God — that He knows what He's doing.

"It also takes a lot of faith in yourself. You have to trust your judgment about something that is *very* important to you. You have to trust your judgment about something that is very different from the way the world sees it.

"Not-so-great people can't do this!"

This sounded true, thought Mark, it *sounded* true.

"And also notice this," asked Father Mike, "trusting your judgment about WHO YOU ARE is an act of your whole self, your whole deepest self.

"This is NOT true about some accomplishment in art or science or sports or politics. Sure, some of these accomplishments are cool enough; but they involve only part of what makes a person who he is.

"And sometimes all the hard work is really motivated by a person's *weakness* — a need for fame, for example — or a really narrow view of what is important — 'nothing matters but winning.'

"WHEREAS, to love yourself is an act of your whole self, and it is motivated by NO weakness.

"In fact, it is *so* hard to love ourselves that if we actually *do* it, and live like we do — not comparing ourselves to others, not caring what others think — well, doesn't that show us we are great?!"

"Can greatness really be that reachable," thought Mark, "can it really be that close."

Father Mike continued: "It makes us great, but the process is not complicated. All it takes is to think things through and say 'yes' to the big picture, the big picture of where we're from, why we're here, and what really matters in the end!"

"So what am I supposed to do now," asked Mark, "to get from all these ideas to a good night's sleep?" Mark knew that this was a good line, and a good question.

"Think about it, Mark," replied Father Mike, "think about the things we've talked about tonight.

"Start with the first thing we talked about. Ask yourself: Has any worldly thing ever made me happy for more than a few minutes? How long will it be before I have to leave everything behind anyway? Is living for worldly things really the way to get ready to leave this world and to go to where I will be forever?

Mark was not expecting to hear about death. "Are you trying to rush me?" he said, only half-kidding.

Father Mike smiled. "No," he replied. "I know at first it's the last thing people want to think about. But that doesn't change the facts of life, and the sooner we start dealing with them, the readier we will be when we *have* to face them. And long before that…if we work for it…we can learn to see how life works as a good thing, a cool journey is with the greatest possible destination."

"So this is the plan, get ready for death?" asked Mark. "Don't I get to live a little first?"

Father Mike smiled. "Of course," he said. "But working for heaven doesn't mean you don't care about your life on earth. It lets you enjoy things *better*, which is exactly what should happen if you are living your life in accord with its purpose, and you see things for what they are. Good things are a glimpse of heaven; they show you what is coming. But you know that they are just a glimpse; you don't expect too much from them; and if you don't actually have them…they feed your imagination and you still get the glimpse!"

"So," said Mark, "what *is* the plan?"

"There are many things you can do to point your life in the direction of heaven," replied Father Mike. "I usually ask people to start with reading."

Father Mike gave Mark a guide to spiritual reading.[1]

"And even before you start reading you might start praying," he said, "and you can start with this:"

THE CHURCH'S PRAYER FOR YOU

We, God's people, make this prayer for you, our brother (sister).

We pray that from the moment you wake up, every single day, you feel the attention and love from God that have also been yours all night long.

---

1 You can easily obtain a copy of this guide for yourself; see the Epilogue, p. 174.

We pray that you know that your life matters, and that as you go forward and help others to do the same, you are making daily an eternal difference. We pray that you understand that you are playing an irreplaceable part in God's plan for us all, and that *you* are preparing to see God as no one else will see Him, except through you forever.

We pray that you often get a glimpse of heaven in the things that God has made—especially in nature, the seasons, and the weather—and in many moments when things are fun, funny, or interesting.

We pray that you have a dream that is also for you a glimpse of heaven, and that you are happy for the hope, grateful for the opportunity, and peaceful with the struggle. We pray that you see your work as love, because this is what it is if this is how you see it.

We pray that you are happy to be tired at the end of the day, and that you love yourself enough to rest, to enjoy your evening meal, and to share your life with others you also love.

We pray that you do share your life with others you love, and that you share your life in conversations that are sometimes endless, just like the life that we will share with God.

And we pray that with time you are only more amazed—that God made *you*, that you will see God, and that God is excited that He will see you.

Father Mike waited for Mark to take it in, then continued. "And if you want us to go over anything we've talked about, or if you have more questions, or you run into something you can't get past, or if you want to share some discoveries...please come back.

"And please come back if you want to talk about a 'next step'...we can do that, too."

"Okay," said Mark, buying time in order to formulate a question that showed that he was really taking seriously this conversation at church: "But how do I know that I'm not just going for 'spiritual' because what I really wanted didn't work out?"

"Well," said Father Mike, "maybe 'material' is what you really wanted in the past, but how is it wrong to think that you have learned from life what is really important, and now you want much more than what attracted you as a kid?

"Besides," Father Mike added, "how is our analysis of what really matters *wrong*?

"Won't there always be a huge difference between what we want and what we can have?

"Isn't discovering who you really are in the eyes of God the best thing you can do right now?

"And isn't it just possible but obvious that God has given you the life you've had in order to make possible this moment?

"Where else are you going to go for happiness and peace?"

* * *

Mark left thinking that this meeting was like nothing he expected. He went home and started praying and he started reading. He found that on his own it was not so easy to get the peace that he was promised. As he was considering the issues, he was often tempted by wishes for something worldly. He admitted to himself the desire that the world recognize him for something great. Peace came when he realized that it is greater not to need the world, and this kind of greatness points clearly in the direction of the life which is really our only hope. ■

IRENE

Irene knew why she made an appointment to see Father Mike. She had felt relief from stress listening to his talk, and she wanted to find out how to keep the feeling. When he asked her, "What can I do for you," this is precisely what she told him.

"What causes you stress?" he asked.

"So many things," she said, "so many things."

"Like what?"

"Oh, I worry about my children. I worry about my parents. I worry about the economy."

"What worries you about the economy?" asked Father Mike smiling.

"I worry that we won't have enough to pay our bills—and then what will we do?"

"Are things OK now?"

"Oh yes, but you never know; and everything is so expensive."

"Tell me about your children."

Irene was happy to talk about her children. One was a teenager and one was almost a teenager; and Irene insisted that they were very good kids, very good. Immediately she pictured her kids doing something well in sports.

"What causes you stress about them?" asked Father Mike.

"Oh, so many things," she said, "accidents and sickness, and there are bad people everywhere." She also thought about sex and drugs, although she did not say so.

"You know, Irene, you parents of today are heroes, NOT because you can protect your kids from every problem, but because the world is filled with so many things you cannot control, and you have and you love your kids anyway."

"There ARE so many things," said Irene, "this is one of the things that causes me stress."

"There are so many things that are not under your control, Irene," said Father Mike, "but this is a reason to feel a certain peace about whatever might happen."

"How can that be?"

"Our job as parents is to do the best we can, the best we reasonably can, to *be* parents—to provide for the needs of our kids, to teach them the right things, to give them the best example we can—and then to remember that they are God's children even more than ours; and He loves them even more than we do; and He has the best possible reason for everything they go through.

"Especially in today's world, Irene," continued Father Mike, "where so much has changed in such a short time. Today, we have to deal with things that people never had before like freedom, and money to spare, and electronic things we are still learning how to deal with! Today, we live in a world with less faith than before, and more disagreement, and less certainty about right and wrong.

"This is the Church's problem, Irene, and God's. It's not your problem in the sense that it's your fault. Your job is just to do the best you can with the special mission that God has given us at this tough time in history."

This was a very grand statement, and Irene was not sure how to react.

"How do I not worry about my kids?"

"I would never ask you not to love your kids, Irene. But I am allowed to ask you to be at peace doing your best. Please remember, our faith says that there is a great reason for everything we go through, and everything our kids go through. In the end, God is getting us ready for a life where things will never go wrong. In the meantime, you are entitled to peace. You are entitled to the same peace that faith wants everyone to have in the face of every situation."

"Even if it's my kids?"

"Yes, Irene, even if it's your kids. Just like you and me, their only real future is life with God. They are going to get there. And they will be loved every step of the way, even if they have to stumble sometimes so they will learn and grow. They will be loved by God and, of course, they will be loved by you."

"It's hard."

"I understand it's hard, Irene. That's why we're talking about it!" Father Mike was still smiling.

"But," he said," allow me to suggest this. It gets easier if we don't see our kids as extensions of ourselves."

"What do you mean?"

"It means that many parents worry doubly about what their kids are doing because they feel that people are going to judge *them* for their kids' sins. Most people don't consciously admit this to themselves, but it is still there."

Irene knew that it was there. She had even imagined herself breaking some bad news about her kids to her parents. She was thinking about it again, right now.

Father Mike continued: "That's why the parents of today are heroes, Irene, because they *have* kids, and they love their kids, even though they know that there is so much that they won't be able to control."

"So what do we do?"

"We do our best. We don't feel we have to do everything. And we leave the rest to God. And one more thing: we try very hard not to think about how anything looks to other people."

"We shouldn't," thought Irene, "but how do we not?"

Father Mike was not finished. "If you don't mind, Irene, very often when people are always stressed…. I know that sometimes it *is* the job; but most often the stress comes from worrying about how we look to other people.

"We come by this naturally. After all, we were made for one another. Practically speaking this means we want people to like us. We want people to like us A LOT. But, if we just go with this feeling and don't think about it, we can easily slip into the mistake of believing that it is the opinion of other people that makes us who we are! Now what others might be thinking about us rules us — it tortures some — almost all the time."

Instinctively Irene thought quickly through a sequence of situations when she remembered feeling almost tortured. The worst was when her mother wondered out loud: "How could a mother let her kids do something like that?"

Father Mike now asked: "You came to the talk last week?"

Irene nodded "yes."

"I don't know if you picked this up, but of all the things that faith wants to give us, love of self was the first and best."

Irene nodded "yes."

"This really is the first thing that faith wants for us, Irene, what faith wants for you: to love yourself for the right reason — because God has made you who you are, and put His whole self into making you you, and no less than He has put into anyone else; and it doesn't matter whether other people can see this or not — right now.

"Other people are human people, Irene. There's lots that they don't see. They don't see who you are inside. They don't understand your part in God's plan. They don't see the person you are going to be when your work on earth is over and God transforms you into the person you are going to be forever. And, besides, other people tend to judge everything according to what suits them. If you make them feel good about themselves, they like you. If not, they don't.

"You don't need to care about the opinions of such people.

"And once you decide that you don't care what others might be thinking, what they might be thinking ceases to affect you. No, people have the power over you which you give them, and *you don't have to give them any.*"

"People have the power over you which you give them." Irene repeated this out loud.

"Of course," said Father Mike, "I know it's easier to say it than to do it. But everyone has their moment. Sometimes it's because something embarrassing has happened, and if they continue to care about what people might be thinking, they know that they'll go crazy. Sometimes it's the opposite. People know that they look good to others, and this becomes too important to them. Now they 'need' something that could change at any moment! One mistake, or somebody just changing their mind about us, and poof, it's gone. Either way, there comes a time when the issue becomes clear and a person has her chance—to believe in *you* because God has made you who you are, and you know you are doing the best you can right now. Is this making sense to you?"

"I think so," said Irene.

"You came to the conference last week. We went over the right reason to believe in yourself. Think it through. God's plan for everything is also His plan for you. Because God is God, He puts infinite attention into everything He does and that includes every detail of His plan for you. It also means He has put no less into you than into anyone else He has ever made or ever will. God wants you to love

His work in you. He wants you to love yourself; He wants you to love yourself as a holy step to loving others better. And one of the best ways to get started is to choose to not care what others may be thinking…and to stop comparing yourself to others. God gave them their advantages and disadvantages to work with; and He gave you yours. Take a stand, at least in your mind. Just be you and don't look around. Am I still making sense to you?"

"Yes," said Irene. "But can I ask you a question?"

"Of course."

"What do I do with my parents?"

Father Mike smiled. "What do you *want* to do with them?"

"I understand what you're trying to tell me," said Irene, "that I'm not supposed to care about what people think…but they are my parents."

"Are they bad to you in some way?"

"No," replied Irene, "in many ways just the opposite. And, maybe, that's part of the problem. I mean… they're good people…but I don't get the idea they think *I'm* all that good."

"Why not?"

Irene was, surprisingly to her, ready with several explanations. She remembered being yelled at when she was trying to help with the cooking. She remembered what her mother said about her as a mother. Most of all, she was bothered by what she did *not* remember — someone saying they were proud of her.

Father Mike listened, and then he responded: "I'd like to offer you two ideas," he said, "one you already know about, and one that maybe you didn't know.

"The first thing is that human parents are human. Just like us they didn't grow up with perfect parents. Just like us there were some things that no one ever taught them; and they picked up some bad strategies for surviving. Just like us they are a long way, in terms of love, from where they will be when God has finished His work with them.

"But we can see this now. And we, as adults, are capable of distinguishing between what our human parents see right now, and what our heavenly parent sees right now. Does this make sense?"

Irene nodded. Father Mike continued: "And one more thing, Irene," he said. "In every person's life, greatness comes when he or she decides to accept themselves for who they are. This is difficult, and it's difficult *whether or not* they have come from a loving home.

"If you didn't get a lot of help to believe in yourself…well, it's obvious how that's difficult.

"But even if you *did* come from a loving home…if you always got lots of support and praise…it means that you were being taught to get good feelings about yourself from the approval of others. No one was trying to hurt you, of course. It's just what happens when people make things easy. If you have a wall to lean on, you lean!

"But if a person wants to be truly secure, and *not* dependent on the approval of others, there comes a time when he or she has to let go of caring so much about what others think—no matter who they may be.

"I know this is not easy, but *you* can do it, Irene, especially if you understand the things we are talking about today. There is no reason that you can't do it. You have as much reason as anyone to believe in yourself for who you are. You can do it. Why not?"

"I want to do it," said Irene.

Father Mike suggested that she think about things, and consider some spiritual reading. He gave her a little book entitled *Why We Look Up*[2] and called her attention to one reflection, "People Have the Power Over You Which You Give Them":

> People agonize over the opinions of others. In order not to:
>
> Think about the people you depend on. You *don't* worry about what they are thinking. You know what they are thinking — for well or for ill — and you live with it just fine.
>
> So who do we worry about? Often they are not even people whom we know. They are people we may never see again. They are people whose opinion we do not respect with regard to any other matter. They are people who do nothing for us, or who are not in a position to do less.
>
> So what are we afraid of? What power do these people have over us?
>
> In fact, they have no power over us except the power we give them — seeking what may be their passing or misplaced admiration.
>
> And we may not even get it. After all, others have their own reasons to see things one way or another. Some people will hate you if

---

2   By the present author (The Crossroad Publishing Company, 2003).

only because everyone else likes you. Some people will speak ill of you if only because you are trying so hard to get no one to speak ill of you. What is worse, one mistake — or someone's vicious lie — and people will never look at us the same.

We cannot assure ourselves of people's admiration. Therefore, we do not need to try. We do better to remember that He who knows us best loves us best, and is preparing us to become who others will see and love in heaven. We do better to remember that the only power people have over us is the power we give them trying to win their admiration. Therefore, once we say it doesn't matter, it doesn't.

Ironically, once we have decided that we do not care what others think, we always impress them.

* * *

Irene's struggle was a tough one because she found it hard to focus on what, exactly, her struggle was. Worry less about the kids? Worry less about the opinions of other people? Worry less about what her parents might be thinking? Finally, she figured it out: she was worried about what everyone else was thinking or doing except one — God. She decided that the best thing to do was to think about what God was thinking and doing — which is loving her for trying hard to do her best. ■

□

HENRY

"I'm here," said Henry, "because I need to figure out what to do."

"What's the issue?" asked Father Mike.

Henry's face got red again just telling his story. He had gotten screwed. That @$$ had gotten away with it. "And off he goes," said Henry, "he got everything he wanted." When Henry said this he had in his head a clear image of his former boss, laughing with people, holding a beer.

"Maybe," said Father Mike, "but I doubt he's happier for it."

"How not?" asked Henry — almost angrily.

"How so?" said Father Mike. "Think about it. A person who would 'screw' you, for the sake of a job, is not a person with much of a conscience."

"That @$$ has no conscience." Henry couldn't contain himself.

"But Henry," responded Father Mike, "conscience is not something that exists in isolation. It is a reflection of a person's spirit. It reflects a person who is very self-centered. It reflects a person with a small spirit. And such a person has small experiences of everything."

"What do you mean?" Now Henry was a little less angry.

Father Mike explained: "A self-centered, small person, a shallow person, doesn't have deep experiences. Like babies they reach for shiny things, like money, but they don't really *enjoy* anything because they don't experience joy. They don't experience peace. Often, because they don't have peace, and are very insecure, they'll do almost anything they think will make them look good. But, of course, this doesn't get them peace. And it certainly doesn't let them be proud of themselves. They look in the mirror at their expensive haircut, but they never see someone they can admire."

"I'm not sure I ever thought of it like that," said Henry.

"It's worse than you thought," continued Father Mike. "If a person is OK taking advantage of other people, how can they afford to think about God?"

Henry made no reply and so Father Mike asked him this in order to keep the conversation going: "Am I correct that you came to my talk last week?"

"Yes."

"Then you understand, I hope, what I mean when I say that such a person couldn't possibly believe in himself for the right reason — because God, out of love, has made him who He is."

"So you are saying that God made this guy to screw me."

Father Mike smiled. "God made all of us to grow up out of selfishness. He made our family to grow into holiness. But the work of the human family can't be easy; it has to require effort. This means that not everybody is going to go forward the same way on the same day. Some people are given more...to lead the way, to be part of the solution and not the problem. God did make that guy, and He loves that guy for who He made him *so far*, even if He wants him — wants us all — to learn from his sins and someday do better."

"So you are saying that it's OK with God that this guy screwed me."

"Not at all. It is not right. It is a sign that this guy has got a long way to go. And because this guy is selfish, he has a selfish, small, and joyless life."

"But God still loves him."

"As a matter of fact, yes, Henry. But don't think he feels God's love. The way we're made, we can feel love only if we are trying to love back. This guy will never feel God's love, he will never feel his own goodness, until he starts trying his best to be good.

"It seems," continued Father Mike, "that for the grand purpose of God's plan you have been given more. You, apparently, have more love in you than would let you do something like this to someone. And this means you are capable of a much richer life inside.

"What is more," continued Father Mike, "if you are able to analyze this situation as God sees it, you can use it to go forward. You can use it as a moment to grasp one of the most beautiful things we teach — that 'faith is its own reward.' The person with more faith not only knows more than other people — where they come from, where they're going, etc. — but because he knows more, he gets the gifts that only faith can give. Do you remember, last week, when I talked about 'the gifts of faith?'"

Henry did remember.

"And even more than that," added Father Mike, "as we are saying, the person with greater faith is a deeper person. Every experience is richer. Colors are brighter. Food is less bland. The person of faith is more alive than anyone without it. And how does the person without faith face death?"

"So what do I do now?" asked Henry.

"You use this situation as your moment. Your moment to understand how 'faith is its own reward' so that you will more consciously receive the priceless gifts... the *priceless* gifts...that only faith can give.

"You use this situation as your moment to let go of the idea that a promotion, money, material things, can make you happy.

"You use this situation as your moment to see how a deep spirit can be happy with less — especially if you took a pay cut at your new job."

"I did," said Henry. And he could have added that the company he now worked for was smaller and offered no way to move up.

"I'm sorry," said Father Mike. "But I am sure that you can still use this situation as your moment to see how a deep spirit can be happy anywhere.

"I am even sure you can use this situation as your moment to be merciful even to your former boss. And, by the way, please understand, by 'merciful,' all I mean is 'understanding.' 'People do the best they can with what they're given.' Since 'faith is its own reward,' and 'the lack of faith is its own punishment,' why would a person who knows better do *worse*? Think of this and JUST DON'T HATE."

"Easier said than done," replied Henry.

"I know," said Father Mike. "But I will be a bit easier if you accept this situation as your moment to decide what you really believe."

"I think I believe."

"I think you do too, Henry, but I also think that we have to face the fact that when most people say 'I believe' what they really mean is 'I'm not against it'; what they really mean is 'I hope it's true.' We know this because if we ask them how their life would be different—what they would do differently—if they *didn't* believe they don't know what to say. What I am saying is that maybe this is your moment to search your mind and heart and see what you see. Maybe it's your time to take a big step forward. You know, we are saying that this other guy needs to take some steps, but this is really true of all of us; and there is so much to be gained if we do. Both now and forever."

Henry was feeling a bit dizzy. He had come to church to talk about the badness of another person, and here he was hearing that maybe *he* had to do better. And it certainly never occurred to him that he could come away from this situation richer. "What do I do?" he asked.

Father Mike gave him a little book entitled *A Faith That Makes Sense*[3] and called his attention to one reflection:

---

3   By the present author (The Crossroad Publishing Company, 1999).

"FAITH IS ITS OWN REWARD"

People of faith are not immune to envy. Sometimes they are especially envious of people without faith, people whose lack of faith permits a life not allowed to them.

To combat such feelings, people of faith need to realize that faith is its own reward. People of faith have so much more than anyone without it.

First of all, they know more. They know where they come from. They know why they are here. They know where they are going when they die.

People of faith know that they are not going to die. They know that they are going to live, to live with God forever. They know that they are going to have all that their hearts already desire — the only place where this can happen.

People of faith know that they are here to grow in the love that prepares them for life with God. Therefore, they have a reason to make a difference in this world, and to live the only kind of life that can make a person happy.

Finally, people of faith know that God is working with them, through everything that happens to them, to prepare them to become the people they were meant to be. Therefore, they have all the reason in the world to accept themselves for who they are, to accept their past for what it was, and to face their future without fear.

If all of this were not enough, faith is the deepest knowledge that we can have. It bespeaks the deepest person that we can be. And every experience of this deeper person is, to that extent, richer. The person with faith is more alive than anyone without it.

"And if you come up with more questions," Father Mike said, "or if you find that something we've talked about just doesn't make sense…or if you see stuff that really does make sense and you want to know more about it, write it down; and then come and see me again."

* * *

Henry did come back. He said that he "liked the things that we talked about last time," but he was "still having a hard time when he thought about that guy — I actually saw him on the street."

Father Mike listened. He asked Henry if it "would be OK if we went back over the stuff we talked about last time?"

Henry said okay.

Father Mike and Henry talked some more about the idea that "faith is its own reward," and "the lack of faith is its own punishment." He reminded Henry that situations like his can be the "moment" that makes us look at things like never before and decide what we *see* about death and life and what to live for. He said that there was no problem going over all this again because this is how we make ideas part of us. "Repetition really is the mother of learning," he said.

"Okay," replied Henry, "but how do I get past these other 'moments'—angry moments?"

"Patience, Henry," replied Father Mike. "And perseverance. Please don't give up. Keep going over it. Look at the alternative.

"Do any of us have any hope apart from what faith offers us?

"Is there anything better than the gifts of faith? Don't many people waste their lives trying to get the gifts of faith from *things*—to feel like 'somebody,' to have 'security,' etc.—when it would be so much easier to get the gifts of faith from faith?!

"And isn't it true that you not only feel *better* but you are *greater* when you live looking at life in the light of faith?

"And, please, Henry give it time. Don't give up. Every day things will get a little bit clearer. The more you look, the more you see.

"It's like looking up at the night sky. When you first go out and look up, you don't see much. But the longer you're out there...you see more and more until the sky is spectacular. It's the same with faith. The more you look at it—going over it again and again—the better you will see the beauty of it." ■

■

GLORIA

Gloria knew why she wanted to see Father Mike. She was hurt, angry, scared, and embarrassed. She felt "empty." The talk she attended gave her a glimmer of hope. Was it a light at the end of the tunnel?

She told her story with more calm than she expected. She was also surprised that it *was* a story with an intelligent beginning that led to an end. She had more to say about how Charlie started to disappear than how things were before that.

Father Mike listened. Finally, he asked, "When you think about Charlie now, how do you feel?"

This question upset Gloria. She could not answer immediately. Finally, she said: "Sometimes I get really angry." There was a pause. "And sometimes, fool that I am, I miss him."

"How many years together?"

"Twenty-seven."

"And there were some good times, I'm sure."

"Yes. But it hurts to think of them now." But, in fact, Gloria was thinking of a couple of good times that often came to mind — a walk in a park just the two of them, their oldest' first Christmas when he knew about Santa. He was so excited the night before.

"Do you sometimes feel you made a mistake to love Charlie?"

"I don't know." This was true, she didn't know.

"I don't think so," said Father Mike. "I'm basically certain you have a big heart, and a big heart sees the goodness that's out there. I'm sure you saw real goodness in Charlie, even though he had some weaknesses you could not have seen until they were tested."

"We were happy, I thought," said Gloria.

Father Mike asked a couple of questions about Charlie. Then he said this: "I have to think, Gloria, that the worst of it is that you feel rejected."

"How do you NOT?" answered Gloria immediately. "I never say it. I never even say it to myself. But yes I feel…" She still could not say it.

Father Mike filled the silence: "For most people, Gloria, it's going to be especially tough when it comes from a spouse, someone you loved, someone you needed to love you back, someone you trusted and showed your true self to like no one else."

Gloria knew that this was true.

"But one thing we've got to get straight, Gloria, when someone does what happened to you, this person DOES NOT speak for God. Even if it was someone you loved and even admired…no one who would do what happened to you is seeing things rightly. What I am guessing is that something went wrong."

"What do you mean?"

"All of us humans are a little weak, Gloria, and, sometimes things happen that pick on our weakness and confuse our judgment and get us to be stupid. In the case of your husband...I don't know — I don't know him — but you did tell me that he recently turned 50."

"Yes."

"Too often, when a man turns 50 he goes a little crazy. When a person becomes 50, the math becomes obvious. There's no way his life is not *at least* half over. He starts to work himself over for all the things he didn't do, and almost certainly will *never* do. He starts to wish he could live his life over; and then he stumbles onto a way to think he can."

"How?"

"It's with a girl, Gloria. Think about it. When I walk down the street, I don't see me, I see the person I am with. And if the person I am with looks young, in my mind, I am young."

"How can anybody believe that?"

"Desperation. And there *is* a little more to it. After all, after twenty-something years with you, there was no way he could pretend to be more than he is. Ideally, this means that he is going to be especially grateful that you love him for who he actually is. But if he hasn't done enough to learn to love *himself* for who he is actually is, he is going to be very tempted to take the easy way out — some young person who is easily impressed by someone with more experience, a little money, knows how to use a credit card. Don't you see that this happens?"

Gloria nodded "yes." She actually thought that it was a little funny.

Father Mike went on. "The crucial thing for you, Gloria, is to understand how it happens, to understand that the fear of dying-a-failure can make even the best person go crazy, and to understand that what he did was based on no clear-headed rejection of you. I have to say...I've seen it too many times...men who have 'rejected' beautiful, charming, virtuous wives because they could not face their mortality. Can you see how this has almost nothing to do with you?"

"I can try," said Gloria, but it sounded as though she was not sure.

"Please, Gloria," he said, "don't be tempted by the awful idea that 'if only' I was more this or more that, he would not have done this to me."

"Isn't it true," responded Gloria quickly; *this* is more or less what she was thinking.

"Well, Gloria, was it you who walked away?"

"No."

"Were you never tempted...did you have no chances?"

"I had chances."

"Was it Charlie's radiant beauty and virtue and talent that stopped you from taking your chances?"

Gloria just laughed.

"So you see," said Father Mike, "it wasn't *his* strength that saved your marriage; it was yours. And by the same token we can say that it wasn't your weakness that let this happen, it was his."

Gloria laugh became a smile.

"Please, Gloria," continued Father Mike, "don't let somebody else's fall bring *you* down. Let it be the opposite. Let somebody's fall be something that inspires you to do one of the best things you will do in your life—to decide, maybe for the first time, to believe in yourself on your own authority, to say 'yes' to God where you know Him best, in His making of you and in His plan for your life."

"This was God's plan for my life?" This was more a complaint than a question.

"I'm sure it seems hard to think so, Gloria," said Father Mike, "but God does have a reason for *everything* we go through, everything. And please remember, everyone's life involves hard things. Everyone's life involves losses, and obstacles, and rejections. But when God asks us to go through these kinds of things, He is giving us a chance to grow. He is giving us a chance to reach down into ourselves and find a deeper, more faithful person than we ever were before. And surely you know that this never happens when things go the way we want. When things go the way we want, we float; we get weak; we get spoiled."

"I guess that's true."

"I don't know why God asked you to go through this particular crisis *now*, Gloria. But I do know that it's part of His plan for you—to give you a chance for a greater *self*-love than you ever had before...because now *you* see the goodness in you, a greater *self*-love than you ever had before...because before you always had help, the attention of somebody else.

"Now is your chance to believe in you on your own authority, and to get the tremendous freedom that you get when you no longer depend on someone else to believe in you for you.

"This is your chance to think things true and make a huge act of faith in you — that you see the truth for yourself.

"This is your chance for a huge act of faith in God — to accept a cross because He sent it, and to take a huge step in the direction of your name!"

"What does that mean?"

"Gloria. Glory. A richer life forever."

"Oh." This was a lot to think about. But Gloria got her thoughts in focus and was able to ask, "So, what do I do?"

"Be with *you*, Gloria. Take advantage of being alone, and be with yourself. Be quiet within yourself and notice your spirit, what a big and deep thing it is. Then talk, talk to God and notice that He is there, with absolute attention to you, and infinite care for how you're feeling. Surely you'll get it, Gloria; if God who is God is paying this kind of attention to me, golly I must, I must be somebody! I must be important, beautiful, loved. Find yourself, Gloria, maybe for the first time. Let this turn out to be the greatest time of your life — 'greatest' in the sense it made you great."

Gloria was thinking.

After a moment, Father Mike added: "And if you need a little more help, besides coming back anytime you want, I would suggest some spiritual reading."

Father Mike gave Gloria his guide to spiritual reading and he also gave her this:

"MY DECLARATION OF FAITH IN ME"

Dear God,

With no one else present…because no one else needs to be present…I declare to You my faith in You and me.

I know that in Your goodness, You have put all You have into making me, and that we will enjoy forever the final results of Your work in me.

For this reason it makes NO difference what others see NOW.

I for my part see that the opinions of others—especially others with whom I do NOT share my daily life—cannot affect me in any way if I choose not to care. Better for me to trust *Your* opinion of who I need to be at this moment in my life, rather than care about the opinions of people who see so much less than You do, and whose instinct is to judge everything according to what suits them.

Besides this, I now see that the attention of others is NOT what makes what we do IMPORTANT, but rather it is *Your* attention; and this is something I have in abundance, and no less than anyone else. Therefore, I declare that I will take my life seriously; I will strive to pay attention to the awesome fact that I exist, and the potential richness of my every experience, and the power of my decisions to form me, and the future glory that will come from every little bit I grow and help others to do the same.

I will NOT waste my life looking at strangers, and talking about what they are doing, as though the actual inner-life of these strangers is somehow greater than mine.

I now see that, at the end of the day, when any of us has the chance to sit down and be with ourselves and experience our lives, the life which we experience...the richness of our thoughts and feelings...comes from nothing else than the depth of our spirit. In other words, I understand that no matter how grand anyone else's life may look, the quality of his or her experience of life is no greater than how much this person has grown spiritually by dealing with what You have sent into his or her life.

What this means is that my life is as great as the attention I give it! I declare, therefore, that I believe in me! I need no one else to agree!

Sincerely,

_____

"You might consider signing it," said Father Mike. "And then print your name on this card:"

My *Real* Identity Card

I, _____,

am a child of God whose life is playing an irreplaceable part in God's plan, and whose spirit will occupy a place in heaven that no one else can fill.

No expiration

(see reverse for Rights and Responsibilities)

This was the reverse side:

Rights	Responsibilities
Feel loved	Love
Have joy	Be joyful
Have peace	Be peaceful

"I have one more question," said Gloria.

"Please."

"If I should accept God's plan for my life, should Charlie?"

"Fair question, Gloria, and I am going to try to give you an honest answer. 'Yes,' God has a plan for Charlie's life, too. And even this time of craziness is part of it. Charlie has entered into a time of making mistakes, and through it, God has lessons for him to learn. I don't know *when* he's going to learn or how far he is going to get. But I do know that just as you are being asked to grow, so is he. And I also know that once he has done the best he could with what he was given, and the death he is so afraid of comes, he is going to be changed—as you and I are, too—and he is going to see things rightly. And this means he is going to tell you he is sorry; and you are going to know he means it." ■

MARY

It was not easy for Mary to make an appointment. It meant that she was going to have to get somebody to watch Dave. Whenever she wanted to do the things she used to do, or just get out, she had to get somebody to watch Dave. "And I tried to tell him where I was going, but I know he doesn't get it!" Now she showed a little anger; and she also "confessed" to Father Mike that she also felt guilty.

"Oh, Mary," said Father Mike, "it's not for me to tell you how to feel, but I hope you don't feel *too* guilty. You have been asked to bear a BIG burden, on so many levels. I mean, you can't come and go like you used to. It must be tiring to have to watch Dave all the time. And maybe hardest of all, you don't have him as company at this time of your life, a time you were probably waiting for for a very long time."

"It's true," said Mary.

"What kind of things were you hoping to do?" asked Father Mike.

Mary started to answer this question. She mentioned a couple of things. "Gardening," she said, "but now I can't even leave the house. Maybe traveling, but he didn't really want to go anywhere — he never did. He never wanted to do anything.

"You see, this is what I am doing," said Mary, angry at herself. "I can't look forward to the future so I only look at the past, and all I see are the bad things. I know it's not right but this is what I am doing!

"What do I do about this, Father? I'm so unhappy."

"I certainly understand, Mary, but I want to understand better. I know it's hard not to be angry with Dave right now, but, as long as we are talking about the past, please try to tell me about some of the good things. How did you meet Dave?"

Mary had met Dave at her first job.

"Do you remember the first time he told you he loved you?"

She did.

"How did your engagement go?"

There were some problems with his family — and hers too — and some funny things happened at the wedding.

"Were you poor when you started out?"

"Oh yes," said Mary who proceeded to describe their poverty with a spirit that actually looked like joy.

"What were your proudest moments with the kids?"

Mary knew immediately how to answer this.

"But, of course," responded Father Mike, "none of it was easy."

"Certainly not," replied Mary still with a smile.

"And I also understand, Mary, that the hardest time is now. But I also know this: God understands, too. He knows exactly what you are going through, and He loves you for it, and is going through it with you."

"But why do I have to go through something like this?"

"Well, Mary, I don't know exactly why God is asking you to go through this, but I know that He knows, and when we see where it will get us, we will be really happy for it."

Mary understood this idea—but she couldn't say she felt it.

Father Mike went on: "You heard me talk about this last week, didn't you?"

Mary nodded.

Father Mike continued. "Now I think it's also true that God has asked a lot from you, a lot. In a sense He has asked you for the greatest thing a person can do—to give up his or her life. Giving up your life is not just about dying. It's about giving up our freedom, things we enjoy, giving up our dreams. But in all these cases we are still giving up our lives, and this has always been the road to glory."

"Would it be OK if I went for a little less glory?" Mary knew that this was a little bit funny.

Father Mike smiled. "Well, Mary, it's not for me to know how great you might become in the eyes of God. But He knows. And He knows what He is doing when He asks some of us for a super-special life. He knows that what we'll get for it *forever* is more than worth what we're paying now."

"It's hard to see this."

"I understand, Mary, but, in some ways your way of greatness is easier than some."

"How?! Please tell me."

"Sometimes people have to give up their lives for people they don't know. This is not true in your case. You know the person you are sacrificing for very well. Over the years he did quite a bit for *you*, I'm sure. You got a whole life, and practiced a whole lot of love, thanks to him. He's not a stranger you have to sacrifice for, or a 'principle' that doesn't even have a face."

"I guess this is true, but I see my friends...they still have the life that I was hoping for, that I was expecting."

"I'm sure that's a little hard to see, Mary, and how good of you to admit it. But let's use this; let's use the fact that you are able to be honest with yourself...that you are able to be 'in touch' with yourself, and to see clearly what you're really thinking and feeling."

Father Mike continued, "If you *are* able to look inside yourself, at what's really there, you will also see that *God* is there. You can experience Him listening to you as you tell Him how you feel. This will make you even more sure that He knows what you are going through and this, in turn, will help you to know that He is going through it with you."

"And if He is going through it with you...well, He certainly wouldn't be doing this unless it were really worth it!

"God knows it's hard, but He also knows it's worth it. Through what He's asking you to do, He's building something in you whose fruits will last forever."

Mary understood that she was supposed to think of heaven, but at this moment this was just not possible.

Father Mike was not finished. "God is giving you a chance...actually, He's kind of requiring you to think things through so you can embrace your faith like never before. And this is a faith that can grow and grow as you keep living it, so you will be ready when finally God takes Dave, or you.

"And even before that...if you embrace your faith like never before, you will find that the sacrifices come easier. And even besides that, you might even find that you can enjoy life much more than you expected. After all, going here and there, and having less trouble with Dave...these things were never going to make you perfectly happy anyway. Something would still be missing. If, instead, you embrace your faith, and use the breaks in your day to dream about the best life you can possibly imagine—in other words, to look into heaven—you will be looking at what you were made for. There is nothing out there that can make anybody happier.

"Is all of this too much?" asked Father Mike.

"It's a lot." How, thought Mary, was she going to be able to think about all this and still watch Dave?

"I know," replied Father Mike. "But to help you keep things in front of you, I always suggest spiritual reading."

Father Mike gave Mary his guide to spiritual reading and this reflection:

"A LETTER FROM GOD TO YOU"

Dear ____,

I am so happy that you are thinking of me because I am always thinking of you.

Perhaps you did not know this. Perhaps you sometimes feel alone, and even unimportant.

Please know that this could not be farther from the truth.

I made you. I wanted to give you life because I knew that I would love you. That means that I also made you different from others — wonderful in a way that I would see nowhere else. Please know I put my whole self into the making of you; I could do no less.

I guess this isn't always obvious, but you don't see you the way I do. You are usually too busy being bothered by your imperfection to see the heart I gave you; and you have no idea of the person I am preparing you to be. (You will be so happy when finally our work is done.)

Please know that I know that life is sometimes very hard. I ask you to trust me: I have the best possible reason to ask you to go through what you are going through — and you will see this soon enough. And I also need you to know this: I am going through it with you. There is nothing you feel that I do not feel, as though it were me, because it is you.

And I am thrilled with all your victories, even those you hardly notice.

And one more thing you need to know: I am so happy when you love, when you give, forgive, and are happy for people, even when they do not know it. I am happy and I am proud because you are imitating the love I have for you, and always will.

Love,
God

"Thank you," said Mary, "I am going to try to see things differently."

"That's what faith is all about, Mary, seeing things differently, seeing things in a better light, the light of the truth about where we come from, why we're here, and where we're going. And one more thing. Nothing that we have talked about today means that you shouldn't try to make things easier on yourself, to look into some practical ways to get a break from Dave. After all, this will help you to be more patient when the break is over. Life is a balancing act; please don't feel bad about your need to get a break."

"Thank you, and I have one more question."

"Sure."

"Why is this mess God's plan for *Dave*?"

"Please understand, Mary, God's plan has count-less effects in the present, and even more as things affect the future. That's why it's impossible for us to know the whole 'why' of God's plan. But I can mention one reason I see."

"Please."

"Dave is paying with the rest of his life to inspire you to shine brighter in heaven." ∎

◘

JOY

J oy had begun to worry that she would never get over it. That was the reason she went to a talk on faith at church. It was the reason she made an appointment to see Father Mike. She had begun to worry that she would never get over it; that was her story. The response to her story was not what she expected.

Perhaps she expected that Father Mike would reassure her that what she was feeling was normal. Certainly he would tell her that healing takes time. Instead, he said this:

"Do you talk to him much?"

"Who?"

"Dan."

"Oh, of course," replied Joy, "all the time. Sometimes I yell, 'why did you leave me?' but I know that that's wrong."

"When you do talk to him…what do you think? Is he getting the message?"

"Oh, Father, I don't know. I don't know what to think. I pray to God, too, to help me somehow, to show me a sign, anything; but nothing happens."

Father Mike smiled. "*This* happened," he said. "Don't you think it's possible that God brought you here, to visit me, for a reason?"

"I hope so, I hope so, so much."

"Good. Let's see what we can do." Father Mike sat a little further back in his chair. Joy did too.

"You know, Joy," said Father Mike, "how we often speak of life as 'work'?"

"Life *is* work," said Joy, thinking of how hard it was to eat alone.

"Okay," continued Father Mike, "you also know, I'm sure, that we often speak of life as a journey."

"Yes."

"Okay," continued Father Mike, "let's put them together and think of life as a business trip. The rest of your life is a business trip; or, maybe better, the rest of your life is Dan's business trip. He is away right now; but soon enough you will be back together. Is this making sense?"

"Yes," said Joy, and, in fact, Dan had made some business trips and so it wasn't that hard to think of herself without him in the house without his having died.

"Now," said Father Mike, "if someone you love is 'away,' you miss him. You miss him for sure; but you are also sure that soon enough he will be back and so you don't feel desperate—and maybe you even do some things you couldn't do if he was around? Am I still making sense?"

"Yes," said Joy; and now she thought of that one time when Dan was away and she made him mad because she cleaned out the garage.

"This, Mary, is how faith wants us to see things when someone has died. We are not expected *not* to

miss him; but we *are* to expect a really, really happy reunion when our work on earth is over, as it will be soon
enough.

"Joy," added Father Mike, "if you can let yourself
be sure that this reunion is coming, the rest of your life
here is going to be really, really different for the better."

"But how can I be sure? How can I be sure about
something like that?"

"You can work for sureness, Joy, and we can do it
together.

"Let's start from the beginning.

"Let us recognize that our faith that God made us
to live with Him forever is everyone's only hope. And,
if this is *somehow* mistaken, then nothing we care about
makes any sense, does it?"

Father Mike continued: "Let's recognize that our
faith that God made us to live with Him forever is everyone's only hope, and this faith follows absolutely from
our experience of God — that everything comes from God
and God is good. How could someone good have given
us life, and to want life as much as we do, if we are not
going to live, and to live with Him forever?

"And how could someone good have asked us to
love people, special people for our whole lives only to
take these people away from us forever?"

"Are you sure?" There was no lack of emotion in
these particular "three little words."

"Actually, yes," said Father Mike, "as sure I can
be about such a big idea as God, and I feel that I am

getting surer every day as I try to live my faith and make it grow; but you don't need to get the truth from me. I think it would be better if you got the truth from Dan."

"How do I do *that*?"

"I already asked you," said Father Mike, "if you talk to Dan and you said 'yes.' Please keep doing it; but do it with this in mind: Dan is with God, and sees what is going on here from God's point of view. He knows when you have something to say. And you can know this: whenever you are thinking of him, he is paying attention to you. Think of this, Joy, and you will experience Dan where he is. You won't see him, but in your heart you will perceive his smile. You won't hear words, but you will get a message. He will let you know that life with God is wonderful. He will let you know that everything is going to be OK. And he will let you know he loves you…more than ever because now he is more capable of love than he ever was before."

"You make it sound so beautiful." "Is this really possible?" she wondered.

"What I want you to do, Joy, is to look for Dan where he is. Let *him* tell you what you need to know. You have probably never known anyone else better; that's true isn't it?"

"Definitely."

"That means that there is no one better to help you see into heaven."

Father Mike continued: "I would imagine you feel you have been suffering more because you had many, many years together."

"Yes."

"Well, you can use this to suffer *less*. You know no one better. You saw the soul of no one better. That's what should give you your best idea of someone in heaven.

"And Dan has been waiting for you to spot him.

"Dan is absolutely alive, Joy. He is aware that we are talking right now, and he will be waiting for you when you get home. Talk to him knowing he is listening. You will experience him where he is. Do it again. And then do it again. Your experience will get clearer and clearer; and you will feel surer, and surer, and surer. Let Dan himself let you know that he is fine. Let him help you start to look forward to life in heaven. Let him give you a freer, richer life here than you ever imagined."

"It would be rich enough not to suffer," thought Joy, but she said, "thank you so much for talking to me, Father. I feel a little hope."

"If you do what we're talking about, you'll get *more* than a *little* hope. Please try it. And please come back if we need to talk again."

Father Mike now suspected that he should ask: "Do you have a computer?"

"No," replied Joy, "I don't know anything about them."

"Then let me give you this." Father Mike went to his papers, picked out one, wrote a couple of words on it and gave Joy "A Letter from Heaven":

Dearest Joy,

First of all, let me assure you, I am not dead. I am with God now, and it is wonderful, far more wonderful than I ever imagined.

Now that I'm here I have to tell you: all those times we felt bad for someone who had died, or said, "I want to go to heaven *but not yet*" — this was crazy. If you could see it, even for a second, you would not want to wait, even for a second, to get here.

When you get here, you'll also see why we had to go through all the things we went through, and once you see what we got from going through what we went through, you would gladly bear a million times more. (I would like to use a bigger word than "millions," but you are not yet able to understand it.)

This you should be able to understand: when you get here you will find that all of us are deeply united in love. Even so, every relationship is still special; and this is especially true of the relationships that we began on earth and which made us who we are. I love you now better than I ever have, and I always will, and we will always be together.

Yours always,

Dan

◩

JAMES

James told his story. He used the word "cancer," but he didn't use the word "death."

Father Mike asked a number of questions about his treatment and prognosis. James responded with phrases like "It doesn't look good" and "The percentages are really low." When Father Mike asked whether they (the doctors) had given him a "time-frame," James said, "A year, maybe two."

Father Mike then asked him about his family, who turned out mainly to be his wife and one brother, and James said that both were "having a hard time with it" but in different ways. "My wife," he said, "cries, and my brother gets quiet."

Father Mike now asked James how he felt (physically,) and James said "Okay." Then he asked how he felt "inside," and James needed a couple of seconds before he said that he was "scared."

"Do you think much about what comes next?" asked Father Mike.

"I *think* about it," said James, "but I don't know. And I wonder if, maybe, there's…nothing."

"Have you thought much about heaven during your life?"

"Not really," said James. "I mean I *heard* about it. It's a nice idea and all that. But I really didn't think much about it." In fact, thought James, it's nice to hope there's something after we die, but isn't this really just wishful thinking?"

"Not even when other people died?"

"When my parents died, for sure," said James, "during the funeral, coming home from the cemetery; but after a while you get used to them being gone and so...maybe they're somewhere, maybe they're not...you go on with your life."

"I'm not proud of this," James added, "but this is what I did. I think it's what a lot of people do."

"Until they can't not face it," ventured Father Mike.

"Exactly," agreed James, and then he said. "I came to your talk. I liked what you said. But...still."

"Still?" Father Mike said this smiling.

"What if it's wrong? I mean, what if it just ends? I mean, you can't come back and...what...try something else? How can we be OK with not-being-sure about something like this?"

"That's a good point," said Father Mike. "So maybe we could go for sureness."

"How do we do that?

"Honestly, James, I think you are going to find out that you were a lot closer to the truth than maybe you thought. The truth that explains the world is all around us. The truth that explains us is written within us. It's just a question of getting people to focus—to NOT live superficially and to really closely look at the world and themselves and see what they see."

"And in your case," Father Mike added, "we have a couple of advantages."

"What?" James had not thought of himself as having any 'advantages' when it came to God.

"Number One, you have to do it. You don't have the option of putting it off for later. You know that every day you look for the truth is one day more to help you find it.

"And Two: We can use what's already going on inside you. I'll bet you are already looking at your-*self* a lot; I mean being conscious of yourself, conscious of you as a thinking, feeling person who knows he's here and who doesn't want to lose his life."

"That's for sure," said James thinking especially about the nights.

"So use it. Keep looking at yourself but, please, James, take the time to notice…the next time you are really conscious of yourself…that your very consciousness is trying to tell you 'There's more to life than what normally meets the eye.' 'I am part of something, not just bigger than me, but greater.' 'I am not alone. When I am thinking, I am not just talking to myself; someone else is getting this.' Am I making sense?"

"Maybe."

"The more you do it, the more familiar it will get, James. And the reason is something kind of simple and very wonderful. Do you remember from last week when

I talked about how faith means that we perceive that the world must come from something greater?"

"Yes."

"That's how God made it. That's how God made us — so that if we look closely at anything we will see the truth of it, that it was made. We can see this when we look closely at anything — the sky, a pen, the house across the street. But we see it best when we look at ourselves. After all, you see things from a certain distance; when you look at yourself there is *no* distance. You are in direct contact with reality, as direct as it gets. You will see that you were made. More than that, knowing God exists, you will experience Him. That's what's going to happen when you recognize the existence of someone who knows everything, including your thoughts right now. Am I still making sense?"

"You might be."

"If you start talking to God, James, you will feel heard. You will know you have God's attention. Frankly, from all you already know about God, who has to be great, who has to be good, you will feel love. Do it again tomorrow and the experience will get even clearer."

"That sounds almost too good to be true."

"Maybe, James, but it's been the experience of people with faith from the beginning. It's my experience — although I'm still working on making my own experience of God clearer and clearer.

"Besides," added Father Mike, "if everything *does* come from someone like God, *shouldn't* it be too good to be true, in other words, better than we can easily imagine?!"

"How do we know we're not just believing what we want to—because we need to believe in something?"

"Well, James, the very fact that 'we need to believe in something'—that our human nature cries out for this kind of thing—already tells us something.

"But, if you're worried about being 'scientific,'" added Father Mike, "please think about what we said last week: science, too, is based on 'just knowing' something basic that cannot be proved—that the world will work tomorrow according to the same rules that made it work yesterday. And if you want to be really scientific, don't ignore your experience. Human experience is that when we look closely at anything our nature tells us that it comes from something greater.

"This, in fact, is our experience of God; and once we experience God, everything else follows. No chance that we were made for death. No chance that we are here for nothing. No chance there is no plan. And it has to be true that we are going to share heaven as a family because that's what love would want us to do…and it's only right anyway since God gave everyone a role in making us us…and the idea of the family makes sense of everything else that we believe."

"I do have a question about that."

"Please."

"Even last week, when you were talking about this idea, that we are going to be one big, happy family in heaven, I had to wonder: how can it be? I mean, how many people are there? I can barely keep track of a dozen. And you are talking about some sort of family of billions."

"Perfectly good question, James. Let's hope I can give you an imperfectly good answer."

Father Mike began: "Already in our life here, in this world, we have the experience that to learn one little thing can suddenly help us to understand something that previously was utterly mysterious. My favorite example is television. I could not for the life of me understand how a picture could be sent through the air until I stumbled onto the idea 'one dot at a time.' Now something utterly mysterious was not only clear but simple and almost obvious. The same thing is going to happen once we get to heaven. The very process of 'getting to heaven' means that God will have to transform us. He is going to make us, the network of memories that *is* us, out of the same 'spirit' that He is made of and then we will be able to see Him, and we will learn more in a moment than we could have learned in a billion years here. Then everything will make sense. We *will be* the family we were meant to be.

"For the time being, you can imagine our family life in heaven in terms of a community or a village where everyone does know and care about everyone else. And where every relationship is special.

"That's how it's going to be in heaven," said Father Mike, "and our relationships with the people who had the most to do with making us who we are going to be *very* special for just this reason."

"That sort of makes sense," volunteered James, "but what about people we didn't like so much, or people that nobody liked?" At this moment James was thinking about the latest mass shooter.

"The transformation of us is the transformation of everybody. Everybody will be much better and brighter than *anyone* was here. People will be sorry for how they hurt others, and they will show it. And people will be much better at seeing it, at forgiving."

"And, yes, everyone will know everything, including things we might feel ashamed of now, but everyone will be perfectly understanding of how all these things were human and how all of us started with nothing, and none of us got very far toward where we're going. It's going to be okay."

"One more thing," said Father Mike, "you don't need to confuse what we say about heaven with questions like, 'My dream is a big house on a hill...but is there a hill in heaven? Do we need a house? Do we eat?' Please understand, James, it's the *experience* of these things that gives the glimpse of heaven. Not the actual house but how it would feel to live in great surroundings, and be filled with great things, and how it feels to win a great victory...." It's the *experience* of the things that gives the glimpse; it's not about the thing itself. Is this making sense?"

"Yes," said James, and he meant it. He felt a spark of hope. "What do I do now?"

"Use what you are already doing, as we said. Get to know God, better and better. You really can get to the point where you will feel His hand out and His arms ready. And, of course, we can keep talking."

"I would like that," said James.

"And please consider spiritual reading," said Father Mike, who gave James his guide.

I will, said James, and then, thinking about that guy he had sort of swindled, he added, "I like what you said about everybody getting forgiven in heaven, but maybe I need to get a little head start." At that moment James had no idea why receiving the love of God makes a person need to make his or her life as clean as it can be. But he was to find out. ■

PART IV:
EIGHT MORE STORIES

HEART TO HEART
(THE STORY OF A HOMILY FOR THE
PURPOSE OF HEALING)

In private, Father Mike had heard enough. So many people were suffering at the hands of others, and he knew that there had to be many more out there. Perhaps they had never spoken about what they were feeling; and this meant that they had never heard what people need to hear. At least they could hear it from him, this week.

He had chosen this particular Sunday because the readings were more in that seemingly endless series of parables of the kingdom. He figured that the people were already pretty well convinced that the kingdom was a good thing, and that indeed the kingdom is coming, or better yet, that they are going to the kingdom.

He opened his remarks quite bluntly. "Today we are going to talk about people who have hurt us."

He went on, "And I am going to start by addressing the feelings of those who suffer the thought that one or both of their parents did not love them.

"This is such a hard thing to bear. It's human nature: Children look to their parents. They look to their

parents for their security in every sense. They look to
their parents to feel secure that they belong, that they are
wanted, that they are loved.

"And when parents are not good at showing this,
because they never learned how, or perhaps because
they themselves were hurt in life and find it hard to love,
their children blame themselves.

"How could children not blame themselves? They
look to their parents for everything. And if my father
or my mother is basically telling me 'I'm not worth
much'…well, what else will I believe?

"We are able to understand this about ourselves.
But we are also able to understand a bigger truth: Each
of us was really made by GOD. Each of us was made by
the God we call Father to be His son or daughter. Each
of us was made by God so He could love us with all His
heart…with all His heart in every case, and this means
no less love in your case. God could do no less.

"We can understand this. And we can understand
that God is God and we are not. We are creatures here
for growing, we are, and very, very imperfect. There is
so much we do not know…so much we do not see…and,
sometimes, our struggles in life confuse us, and we do
not see things at all! This is sometimes true of me, and it
is also sometimes true of my parents.

"We can understand this. We can understand that
our human parents do not decide our worth; God does.
And through our faith we can learn to see ourselves as
He does. And we can understand that, one day, when
God has finished with His work with us all, our parents

too will see us as God made us. And they will love us, and be good at letting us know it.

"I can say the same about our children." Father Mike was changing the subject. "Sometimes it's not our parents who don't seem to love us; it's our children. And sometimes they even blame you for it."

Some people were nodding.

Father Mike went on, "And the thing that hurts worse is that sometimes you believe it.

"Here's something else we can understand. You can always make parents feel guilty because no one ever does a perfect job. Which of you is other than human? Which of you was raised perfectly by *your* parents? Which of you saw the future coming, and was perfectly prepared to deal with so much stuff that you never experienced?

"This is what I recommend to you: Ask yourself what I ask myself: Did you do your reasonable best? Did you do the best you could with the tools and the time and the situations you were given to work with? What would you have done differently—that was obvious at the time? Was your bottom line your kids, or some sin that you were into? That's what God was looking at, and that's what your kids will see when God has finished His work with us all."

Father Mike was not yet done.

"Now I would like to speak to anyone who might have been hurt by a peer—a friend, or more likely a spouse, maybe now an ex-spouse."

Now there was some rustling in the pews.

"Please face the possibility that you are angry because you feel rejection, because once you face it, you can throw the idea out.

"Now," said Father Mike, "I get to say one of my most favorite things: 'Your rejection is always the other person's fault.'

"Now, by 'fault' I don't necessarily mean something that other people should feel guilty for. No, I mean 'fault' in terms of the original meaning of the word— 'something missing.' In this case, I'm talking about what they don't see.

"Think about this," continued Father Mike, "the person who knows you best loves you best. You know, of course, that we are talking about God who made you so He could love you with all His heart forever, and sees right now the beauty of the spirit that you and He are making into this person.

"Please, don't be thinking, 'No, it was my *fault* that somebody rejected me…because I was bad…because I did this…because I never did that….' Maybe so, but God never stopped loving you. Even if you tried to make it hard…God never stopped loving you. Anyone who *did* stop, didn't see what God sees.

"Please, I'm NOT saying that some other person is bad, or that they lied when they said 'I love you.' But he or she didn't see what God sees.

"What God sees inspires Him to love you as much as He could love anyone.

"And now we have one more thing to talk about.

"I need to speak to the people, who are almost certainly out there, who have been subjected to sexual abuse."

Just barely there was an audible gasp.

"You are not alone, but I know you feel alone.

"Besides abuse itself, this is the terrible thing that happens. So often, when children are abused...there are many things they don't understand, but instinctively they feel ashamed. They keep what happened inside. They don't talk about it with anyone—many times they don't even know how to talk about it—and so they never hear the two things that a person who has suffered abuse needs to hear: you are not guilty. And you are not dirty.

"You are certainly not guilty. No child is ever guilty of the evil choices of an adult, especially an adult who might have had authority over them. Children don't understand what is happening. They don't how to stop it. Too often what happens is that they grow up and judge themselves as they learn more—they judge themselves when they are twenty for what they didn't do when they were eight!

"No," said Father Mike with force, "you are not guilty.

"And you are not dirty. What makes you dirty is what you choose. You did not choose what happened. You did not want it. You were not 'into' it. In your mind you were screaming 'stop it.' Yes, in your mind, you have a terrible memory. But this memory says nothing about you; it says nothing about your goodness as a person. This memory does not define you!

"You are not dirty. And you are not guilty."

Father Mike's tone changed again. "I realize that not everyone needed to hear what we have talked about today," he said. "Not everyone needed to hear it, but everyone might need, someday, to say it, to talk about these things with someone who has confided their feelings to you…."

Now Father Mike did what he always did and made a quick summary of the points he hoped he had shared. Then, as always, just before the action at the altar, he tried to link his points to the meaning of Mass. "Remember, we are now going to see…once again presented live…Jesus accepting the cross. We are going to remember his rejection…at the hands of people he wanted so much to please…for whom he had tried to do so much…. We are going to remember his betrayal and abandonment, and the hideous abuse to which his body was subjected. And we are remembering how he conquered all this by accepting it, and made his way to glory. And you can do it too." ■

◘

LUZ
(HAS BEEN UNFAITHFUL IN HER MARRIAGE)

Irene, her neighbor, talked so much about her meeting with Father Mike that Luz figured she would give it a try. Luz needed to do something. She had fallen into a deep, dark hole. Luz was nervous when she got to Father Mike's rectory. She introduced herself and she started her story.

It had started as these things so often do. A middling marriage that had begun to suffer from creeping indifference. Growing apart from a husband, a good husband and a good man, who had never been much of a talker and was not that good at showing interest.

Through a connection at work, Luz had gotten to know someone who showed her (and stirred in her) more "interest." It got to be clear that he was interested in Luz. This made Luz feel good about herself. And bad.

Her long talks with her "friend" continued. Certain things were said. A couple of lines were crossed.

And now Luz found herself in the deep end of the pool, and confused and scared.

Her story was not hard to understand. Father Mike did not need to ask many questions. He did ask this: "Do you love your husband?"

"Yes," said Luz.

"Do you want to save your marriage?"

It took a second for Luz to say, "I don't know."

"I understand," said Father Mike. "But, may I ask you: do you feel that your marriage ought to get your best efforts to save it?"

"Yes." Luz was able to answer quickly. "I know that's right."

"Okay," said Father Mike, "do you think there is any chance you can recover your love for your husband while you are still communicating with your friend?"

"Probably not."

"Probably?"

"No, I know I can't."

"You've probably tried before."

"Yes. A couple of times. But he calls me, and the feelings come back, and I just can't walk away. This is the problem."

"It *is* a problem Luz, a very human problem. But there is something about us humans you need to know. When we spend time with almost anyone, and get even a little close to this person, bonds are formed, and it will always hurt when these are broken.

"I've seen it on airplanes!" explained Father Mike. "People start talking; they share a little of their story, and three hours later when the plane lands, they are exchanging information they will never use because they can't quite bear the thought that they will never see this person again!"

Finally Luz managed a smile of her own.

"What I am trying to say is that for you to say 'no more' to your friend is going to hurt, but that doesn't mean you are making a mistake. It's going to hurt, but this doesn't mean that you can't do it. It's going to hurt, but the hurt will pass. It's like ripping off a bandage. It hurts when you do it, and for a little while afterward, but the pain does go away."

At this moment Luz could not imagine the pain going away. All she could think of was how hard, how painfully hard, it was going to be to walk away from this relationship that conflicted with her marriage. "What did I do?" she said. "What did I do?"

"You found out how fragile the human heart is," said Father Mike. "You found out that relationships never stop needing care. You found out why it's necessary to be a little scrupulous when it comes to the rules in a marriage."

"I think so."

"Do you think you can do what we are talking about?"

"I think so."

"Can I give you one more piece of advice?"

"Of course."

"If you really want to end this thing with your friend, you will have to stop talking to him. Period. Intimate talk—and any talk with him now counts as intimate—*generates intimacy*. Just talk about 'your feelings' and your feelings will get stirred up. Talking about 'our relationship' ensures that you still have one. The only thing to do is tell him your decision, and ask him to support you; and if he does not respect what you have asked—what does that mean? What does it tell you about *him*?! If he tries to get a conversation started, just repeat back the same sentence: 'Respect my decision.' Or 'No more conversations.' Or whatever single sentence comes naturally to you."

"I understand," said Luz. There was a long silence, then she asked, "Will God forgive me?"

"Absolutely," said Father Mike immediately. "Please, Luz, try to look at things from God's point of view. None of us is born knowing everything. Actually, each of us is born knowing just about nothing and being very selfish! None of us gets perfect help to grow up fast without any problems. None of us is perfectly prepared to face every situation we've never faced before.

"Life is about taking steps and learning. And when we learn from a mistake, we turn a bad thing that we did into a good thing that we now know, or know *better*. We are *more*, not less, for what has happened.

"That's what God sees. He is thrilled that you learned and so, of course, He forgives you. But, in return, He asks for something. Actually, He asks for two things—wisdom and compassion."

Luz knew that Father Mike was going to explain what he meant.

"By wisdom," he said, "we are talking about what you've learned about life, about relationships, about rules…. We need to remember these things for the sake of the future."

"For sure," said Luz.

"And by compassion, we are talking about compassion for people who have not yet learned what you are learning now. What God does *not* want is for you to learn more and then use it to despise others."

"I understand," said Luz.

* * *

Luz did understand. She did her best. After one false start, she made a break with her friend. She suffered over it for a while, successfully hiding it from her still disinterested husband, and got past it. She saw Father Mike again, and he suggested some ways for Luz to approach her husband with the goal of building a richer marriage. Slowly, but surely, they did. ∎

◉

JOHN
(IS STRUGGLING TO FORGIVE INFIDELITY)

J ohn didn't see it coming until she'd confessed it. He himself had flirted around, and almost done more; he couldn't imagine her doing the same.

This was a double standard and John knew it, but he couldn't get past it; so he went to see Father Mike.

"How does she explain it?" asked Father Mike.

"She says I stopped paying attention to her," replied John. "And there was this guy from her job—I can't even say his name—and he's divorced, and he does pay attention to her. And one thing led to another, until…I still can't believe it."

"Does she say it's over?"

"Yes. She even quit her job—at the time I didn't understand why."

"And she has no communication with this guy?"

"She swears she doesn't."

"Does she say she's sorry?"

"Oh yes. And I believe her. I mean…she told me on her own. I didn't suspect anything."

"Do you believe her explanation about what happened?"

"I guess so. And I guess some of it's true — I wasn't paying attention to her like before; and I didn't get it when she tried to talk to me about it. I didn't think it was that important."

"Are the two of you talking now about how to make things better?"

"We're trying — but it's hard. I mean…sometimes I think about things and I blow up…and she takes it…but it's doesn't help…and that's why I'm here."

"I guess you are picturing her with another person, and imagining how much she thinks about him."

"YES."

"This is a tough thing, John," said Father Mike. "You want to change the past, and you just can't do it. That would frustrate anybody."

"What do I do, then?"

"Let's look at what we've got. We've got the fact that all of us are human and we are sometimes weak and we make mistakes. We got the fact that our job here on earth is to learn from our mistakes; and when we do it we are *more* than we were because of our mistakes, not less."

"How can cheating on me make my wife *more* of anything good? I don't look at her the same way. I just can't."

"I understand how you feel, John, I think," said Father Mike; "but sometimes what we love in another person is our *idea* of who they are — it's really our idea of who we want them to be. But nobody really IS this. People are people, and there is weakness and foolishness and selfishness in us all. Now, maybe, in *both* of you, there's a little less of all of this. In this sense you are *more*."

Father Mike continued: "I always say this and I have seen it often: you can come out of this with a better marriage than you ever had before. This can happen if this situation has taught you things you really needed to know: Now you know how important this other person really is to you. Now you know how important it really is to do what marriage is supposed to be—two people sharing their lives, their thoughts, their dreams. And now I'm sure you know how important it is to have rules."

"It's hard." This is all that John could say.

"I know it's hard, John," said Father Mike, "and I'm sure the hardest thing is thinking about her memories."

John just nodded.

"But," continued Father Mike, "you can think of this: if she made a mistake and is really sorry about it—and you said that you see she is—she doesn't have *happy* memories about what happened. Thoughts about what happened make her sad; they are embarrassing. She doesn't want to think about these things, ever. She doesn't want to think about these things any more than you like to think about some of the things in your life that you are…not proud of. Weren't there some of those, John?"

Unavoidably, John thought about the last one.

"Your wife won't be thinking happy thoughts about what happened. She won't be thinking about it at all—unless you bring it up."

"So, what do I do now?"

"Please, think about what we have talked about. Get it clear in your head that life is about learning from mistakes; it's the job of us all.

"When we learn we are more, not less, because of what has happened.

"When something like what happened to you happens, the person who offended their marriage can come out of it more sure than ever that they love the person they hurt.

"The other person...in this case, I mean you...can find in himself a truer love than you ever had before. You can discover that you love her because she is *her*, and not because she is everything you wanted *her* to be.

"The two of you can figure out better ideas about how to care for your marriage...not only how to save it, but to make it a better marriage than you would ever have had otherwise. This can happen!

"It *will* happen if the two of you talk about good things—the good things you still see in each other, and your good memories, and your hopes about the future.

"And one more thing," said Father Mike. "When something like this has happened, the other person has an opportunity to do something that some people never get around to. Some people spend their whole lives depending on the attention of somebody else for their sense of worth. But our worth really comes from the God who made us, and who put all He has into doing it—no less than He has put into the making of anyone else. The job of other people is to *confirm* God's work. It's nice if they are good at it. But even if they aren't, your worth is still there. If this situation teaches you to see this, you will feel less hurt than you do right now, less hurt because you will feel less desperate to have her adoring attention all the time. If this situation teaches you to believe in yourself, you will worry less and less about the opinions of people around you, and you will feel freer around other people for the rest of your life. Please, John, your main work now is to believe in yourself like never before, for the right reason, because God has made you who you are so far."

John left Father Mike with hope. Father Mike had hope as well. Still, he knew that if he did not hear from John again, this could be either a good sign or a bad one. ■

PHIL
(IS DRINKING TOO MUCH)

Phil was Mark's friend. Phil was drinking too much, and having real trouble with his wife over it. Mostly to appease her, he agreed to do something about it. What he did was to see Father Mike.

According to Mark, Phil was drinking too much but didn't have a problem. According to Phil, half of it was his wife's problem; she was overreacting.

Father Mike had a couple of questions. "So when you have these fights, you usually have at least a buzz, right?"

"Yeah."

"And pretty much every time you have something to drink, you get at least a buzz?"

"Usually, maybe, but not always."

"And you have something to drink pretty much every day?"

"I have a stressful job. I come home in traffic. I like to have something to help me relax."

"Would you say you *need* it, Phil?"

Phil had to think. "No. I wouldn't say I 'need' it. I like it. It helps me relax."

"Okay. How many before you feel the buzz?"

Phil had to think about this. "Maybe three," he said.

"I have to ask you, Phil, are you aware what a buzz really is?"

"What do you mean?"

"A buzz is alcohol running around in your head trying to convince you to have more. It's chemical. Past a certain point, the 'feel good' feeling takes over your brain and all it knows is 'more is better'; and that's when one thing leads to another, and another, and…you get what I mean, don't you?"

"I guess so."

"Now, if a person has a problem, he's looking for that 'feel good' sensation even before he drinks. Alcohol has already changed the chemistry in his head. He's been getting so much alcohol so often that it's part of his system. Now he needs it."

"I don't need it."

"Okay, Phil, let's find out. This is what I suggest. Pick a day. Better yet, start tomorrow. Declare that 'two' is your limit. Take your time with them. If you get to bed without breaking your rule, not even topping one off, mark it down. Mark it on a calendar. 'A' you kept your rule; 'F' you didn't, even if you came up with some 'reason' that today was 'special.' Do it for two weeks and come back and show me your calendar. If you have almost all 'A's, it looks like we win. If not, we might have to face the fact that there is a problem, and it's not smart for you to drink at all. And if you *can't* do that — *can't not drink* — then we'll have to look at a more serious plan. Does this seem fair?"

"I can do it."

"Will you do it?"

"Sure."

"Will you come back in two weeks?"

"Sure."

"Great. One more thing. If, Phil, you find out that you *can* do it, but that *not* having a buzz leaves you feeling stressed or nervous or something like that, please make sure we talk about it. A lot of times people start going after that regular buzz because they're just not at peace within themselves. They think the pressure is from others, but it's really pressure they're putting on themselves. Or maybe it's that life is a little empty and we just have to fill it with something, at least a distraction. Or maybe there's some serious issue from the past, and this is how we *don't* think about it. This is where faith comes in. *You* come in and we can talk about it. There is nothing that faith can't handle. There is nothing that faith can't help us see differently, better.

"Let's look at the next couple of weeks as an experiment. We're going to find out how Phil can go forward, go forward to a better, deeper, more peaceful life."

"I can do it."

Phil went home and got buzzed. The next day he got an "A" and was happy to mark it down. Within a couple of days he cheated some but still gave himself an "A." By the middle of the next week he stopped marking his calendar. He did not go back to see Father Mike.

* * *

Two days after Phil did not show up for his second appointment, Father Mike, who had asked for Phil's e-mail address, sent him this. It was supposed to be printed, cut out, and turned into a two-sided card:

Why to Stay Sober

Because people love you, and there is nothing better than a sober life with people who love you.

Because God loves you—and this means that your spirit is beautiful, that your life's struggle is important, and that your life with God will be wonderful.

How to Stay Sober

Be conscious of what you are doing and don't believe any of your excuses not to keep your rules. Remember, believing an excuse is a sign of the problem.

Remember, temptation is chemical; it will pass if you are strong, but not so the consequences if you are not.

■

MIRIAM
(FINALLY ASKS FOR FORGIVENESS)

Miriam had gone to Father Mike's talk. Lately she had been going to a lot of things at church.

This was new, because her life as a young woman, a pretty and quite modern young woman, had not involved a lot of time in church. Her parents made sure she had covered the bases, communion (and confession) and confirmation, but it was never interesting then, and it got less interesting as she got older.

Eventually, she got married — not in church — and now she had children. She wanted them baptized and so she had to go back to church for some kind of classes. They were not what she expected.

Father Mike, who gave the classes, gave her the idea the he was someone she could talk to — she felt that he would listen, and almost sure that he would not yell. She could not have been more stressed out the night she walked into his room for appointments. "My name is Miriam," she said. "I am very nervous."

"With me?!" responded Father Mike with a smile. And then he added, "You know that God already knows whatever it is you want to talk about. And you know that He is only proud that you are here. I will do my best to represent Him."

"It's just...I didn't used to go to church very much. I was never religious or anything. And now I've started going, and I am learning a lot, a lot of things I never knew...and there are a lot of things I never thought about." Here Miriam had to gather herself.

"Take your time," said Father Mike.

"I mean," continued Miriam, "you grow up, you see how things are, you do what everybody else does." Another pause. "And this means you do some things you are not proud of."

"Is that why you are here, Miriam?"

"Yes."

"Then please remember this: God already knows everything you have in mind, and He understands; and all He wants is that we grow through it."

It took Miriam a few more moments and then she continued: "The first time...there was this guy; and he said he loved me; and I was only a teenager; and I had no idea...." Still another pause. "And I came out pregnant...." And now Miriam started to cry.

Father Mike had tissues handy. He didn't say anything right away. When finally Miriam used her tissue, he said, "It's so good that we are talking about this, Miriam; and we are going to get past it."

Miriam continued crying.

Finally, Father Mike asked her, "You wanted to tell me that you didn't have the baby?"

Miriam tried to nod. She cried some more and then she said, "That guy who 'loved' me just took off — I told him I was pregnant and he just hung up, and then he wouldn't take my calls. And I was so young…and I thought 'I have my whole life ahead of me; I just can't lose it like this!' And I didn't think about what I was doing, really…I didn't know about God, I didn't know about anything."

"Did it ever happen again, Miriam?"

Miriam started to cry again; and then she said, "Two more times. It was the same thing. Somebody said he loved me — and I wanted to believe him. And then…. I had already done it before; and I thought 'This is what you do to get out of trouble.' I know it's terrible, but I didn't think about God. I didn't know so many things I know now."

"I know that's true, Miriam," said Father Mike. "And you came to see me so you could say that you are sorry."

Miriam said "yes" like she had never said "yes" before.

"Then I need you to know, Miriam, that God forgives you. He understands everything that you just told me. And He knows that you are sorry. And the fact that you came tonight so you could say it…He thinks that this is beautiful."

"How can He forgive me?"

"Because you're sorry, Miriam."

"That's all I have to do?"

"And learn from what happened. Which you have. You said it yourself: you weren't raised to be really sure that certain things were really wrong. And NOBODY is born with all the wisdom and strength they need in order to do the right thing every time."

"I did it more than once."

"Yes, Miriam, and you also fell down more than once when you were learning how to walk."

She nodded, and wiped her eyes.

"And you had to be corrected more than once when you were learning how to talk. Life is hard, and growing up is hard; and wisdom and strength never come easy. Sometimes we learn the first time; sometimes it takes longer; but the great thing is that we learned.

"And think of this, Miriam," added Father Mike, "when you learn from a mistake, you turn a bad thing that you did into a good thing you now know. Now you are more not less because of what has happened.

"When God looks at you, this is what He sees. He doesn't see someone doing something bad; He sees a young woman who is now filled with a deep idea of right and wrong, and a deep desire to live the holiest life she can. Right?"

Miriam nodded—vigorously. But then she asked, "But how do I live with this? I mean I always thought about it—even before—but now that I know better… when I see my children, when I see any children…."

"Please understand, Miriam, God would never leave the destiny of any of His children in human hands.

Every little life is in *His* hands. They had their purpose. And although I can't tell you the whole story of why all this happened—I'm not God, I don't see the future—I can tell you some good has already come out of what happened...it's happening right now."

Miriam closed her eyes, but she was listening.

"Now you are deeply convinced about what sex and commitment mean. Now you are deeply convinced about the sacredness of every human life."

Miriam nodded, and put her face in her hands.

"And now, I hope, you have begun to believe that you should loved for *who you are*—and NOT because you behave the way somebody else wants. God wants this for you, Miriam—not just that you accept His forgiveness, but that you come out of this convinced that you are loved. This will inspire you to live the best life you can for the rest of your life.

"Is this making sense?"

"Yes," said Miriam, "but what do I do now?"

"Feel forgiven," said Father Mike. "Know that God does not want you to live in shame. Feel loved. Be grateful. And spend the rest of your life trying to give back. Can you do that?"

With conviction and gratitude Miriam said "Yes!" ∎

◘

CATHERINE
(HAS LOST A SON WHO TOOK HIS LIFE)

Catherine came to see Father Mike because she liked his preaching and because several of her friends said that he could help.

Catherine had lost her son, Kelvin, to suicide.

She had been devastated. Even now, as a person of her generation, she did not understand how growing up in front of the rich and famous on television had given her son expectations that real life was never going to be able to realize.

She had known that he was smart, but she did not understand how being brighter means a person has a greater capacity for suffering.

She had known a little about how he was bullied in high school—there had been a couple of calls from the principal—but she did not understand how the bully could be transferred out but the wounds would remain.

She had known that by graduation Kelvin was not really excited about anything except, maybe, money so that he could buy the electronic stuff that everybody else had their faces buried in, and get a ticket to what everyone else was going to. (For him, at least, clothes weren't much of an issue.)

She had known he hated his job and his boss, because he said so; and when she tried to get him to think about going back to school he mostly made excuses and talked only vaguely about the future.

She had known Kelvin liked some girl at work; but she did not know how much; and she did not know that this girl liked somebody else who was a lot "cooler" than Kelvin.

She had seen that Kelvin was going through a bad time. His explosions of anger at the slightest provocation had given way to quiet and isolation and an inability to look her in the eyes.

But she had had no idea that Kelvin ever used any drugs until he overdosed on purpose. She knew it was on purpose because the note he left said: "Screw the world."

Now Catherine was filled with terrible feelings. She missed her son, of course; and she was also afraid for his soul; and she also felt very, very guilty for what she had not done to save him.

This last thing was the first thing that she said to Father Mike.

"First things first, Catherine," he replied. "Kelvin is with God. He will never feel pain again. I know this is really, really hard to imagine, but let me assure you: your son is healed and he is happy."

Catherine tried to remember the last time Kelvin had seemed really happy. It meant thinking back a number of years, but she got a picture in her head and tried to hold it.

"Life here is hard for everyone. It was especially hard for him, and now his work is over."

"What work did He have? What did he accomplish? I can't..." Now the happy memory was gone, and replaced by the look of frustration and futility she remembered from his face.

Father Mike spoke slowly and cautiously. "The work of each of us, Catherine, is to deal the best we can with what God sends us. Through this struggle a seed is being fashioned within us. And when this seed becomes what God needs it to be He takes us—and He transforms us."

"Are you saying God *sent* Kelvin all the things that hurt him so much?"

"Well, Catherine, our faith *is* that God is behind everything, and that everything He sends He sends to get us ready to live with Him forever. I know it's sometimes hard to see this...."

"Yes, it is!"

"Let's use the example of an actual seed," continued Father Mike. "You cut it open, you look inside, and you don't see a little flower; you don't see a little tree. What you see makes no sense until the seed grows into what it was meant to be. Then you see how this or that turned into something wonderful that was in no way obvious when the thing was just a seed. But to become something greater, the seed has to disappear."

"Besides this," said Father Mike, "we are all part of God's family. The things that happen to us are also supposed to affect others. What Kelvin went through is affecting a lot of other people."

Catherine nodded to that.

"And I know that those effects might be pretty rough right now. But the story doesn't end here. Kelvin has changed and is changing you. And from all that you've been going through, surely you realize he is making you deeper.

"Besides you, other people might be learning more kindness and compassion, by thinking of how they treated him, and what happened.

"And there will be many other effects that will make the human family forever richer, that we will we someday see."

"But he was so young," said Catherine, "he had his whole life in front of him."

"Please, Catherine, I know it's not easy to hear this — it's not easy for me to say it — but Kelvin didn't have his whole life ahead of him. If he was meant to live a long life here, he would have. Instead, God had a different kind of mission for him; and this mission has been accomplished."

At this, Catherine simply broke down sobbing. Father Mike didn't try to stop her. She recovered herself, and he handed her some tissues.

"Catherine, I know not having Kelvin here with you is a loss you never imagined having to face. And I believe that you would give your life so he could have his back."

Catherine had already thought this — many times.

"But be assured: life with God is SO much better than life here. No one who sees God would say that they wish they could have had few more years on earth. Life with God is what we are made for. What is life here if this is not true?!"

"You say that Kelvin had a mission. I was taught that what Kelvin did was a terrible sin."

"I know you were taught this, Catherine, but that was when we saw things a little too simply. Back when people were simpler, and saw almost everything as black and white, they thought 'If God is the Lord of your life, then *He* decides when you go. If you, instead, reject the life *He* gave you…well, this is a serious sin.' But," continued Father Mike, "now we know that no one who successfully takes their own life was trying to reject God. They were trying to stop the pain. They HAD TO stop the pain. The example I always use is this: if someone puts a gun to your head and says 'don't breathe for three minutes,' even if you believe him, you are going to breathe before three minutes. You have to stop the pain.

"You can also think of it this way: all of us leave this life because something fails. Sometimes it's my heart, sometimes it's my liver or my kidney, and sometimes it's my head.

"And as long as we are talking about pain," added Father Mike, "I believe that sometimes when someone is going through something like you are going through, one of the worst things that happens is that they replay in their mind, over and over, the terrible moment the person they love did something terrible."

"Oh this is true," said Catherine.

"But, please, Catherine, that moment is OVER. Kelvin doesn't experience it again and again every time you think of it. What he *does* experience is the sight of God; and now he knows that what he got was WELL worth the pain he paid to get there. You yourself have been through painful things that are now past, and were necessary to get you where you are.... Where Kelvin is there is no trace of pain. There is only joy, all the greater for what he endured to get it."

"I need to talk about one more thing," said Catherine.

"Of course."

"Shouldn't I have seen this coming? I mean...I saw that things were going wrong, and I didn't do anything about it—except to nag him and..." and now there were tears.

"I guess things are clearer *now*," said Father Mike, "but isn't that always true when we look back on things? But at the time, do you ever remember thinking that something like this could happen?"

"No," replied Catherine, "I never imagined it. I mean...I would have talked to Kelvin more."

"My guess is that you never had an experience with anything like this before."

"Never!" said Catherine, "except what you hear about."

"So now if you know more, Catherine, the value of that knowledge is to help others, and not to hurt yourself. Please."

"What do I do now?"

"Talk with Kelvin."

"Oh, I try to...but I don't know what to think...if he hears me...what he thinks...."

"I hope you know a little better now," said Father Mike. "You know where he is. You know he is healed and happy. And not only does he understand what happened to him, and why it had to be part of the big picture, he actually sees *everything* from God's point of view. This means that he knows we are talking about him right now. It means that when you go home and think about him, he knows that too. Do it—think about Kelvin knowing that at the very same moment he is thinking about you, and you will experience him where he is. You will experience that he is alive, and changed, and all you ever hoped that he would be. Let him help you know that life with God IS our future, and it is the place where the two of you are going to be reunited once your mission on earth is accomplished."

Catherine got up to go. She felt somewhat spent, but somehow less alone. ■

◘

BRIAN
(IS SUFFERING DEPRESSION)

It had not been easy for Brian to ask for an appointment. It's not that Father Mike seemed difficult to talk to. Quite the contrary, Father Mike seemed easy to talk to. But this was the problem. Father Mike seemed like a relaxed and happy person; he was cool. And, now, Brian felt very uncool.

For a few weeks now — how many, he had stopped counting — he had been battling this weird, terrible sadness. It had come upon him out of nowhere, he thought, and now it was relentless. Though he had been able to keep it to himself, he felt it all day long, and it got worse when he was alone. Then it felt like a knife in his head. He wanted to cry, or at least to cry out, but he could not.

And the pain got worse when he looked forward. When he looked forward, he saw nothing. His future was just darkness. He could not see himself doing anything he would enjoy. Everything he thought of made him feel…hopeless…desperate…stuff like that.

And he was battling not just sadness, but also fear. And this too was getting worse. As the days had gone on, he was finding himself fearful of doing even the simplest things. Sometimes the thought of taking action was almost paralyzing. Even though, when the moment came, he had been usually able to do what was needed, this always came as a surprise. He wasn't sure how long he could go on.

This is what made him accept that he had to talk to someone. He picked Father Mike because he knew him. He got a 7 p.m. appointment and he arrived early, waited in his car, and was internally trembling as he got to the door.

Father Mike's study was a comfortable room, but Brian was not comfortable. He introduced himself and said, "I don't know where to start."

"Just start," said Father Mike, "and if there's something I don't understand, I will ask."

Brian started to tell his story and he tried to explain how he was feeling. He found that words came easier than he'd expected. Here and there, Father Mike interrupted him with questions:

"When did this start? Was there something difficult going on in your life then?"

"Not really" was the response.

"How do you sleep?"

"Pretty good," said Brian, showing the surprise he already felt when he thought about this.

"And when you first wake up, do you feel pretty good for the first few seconds, and maybe think that finally this is over until it comes back over you like a cloud?"

"Yes!"

"You said that you're becoming afraid to do things. Are you talking about things that you had no problem doing before?"

"Some."

"And let me ask you about the sadness," said Father Mike. "Does it hit you all over again whenever you focus your mind on something…like a tree changing color, or a house on a hill, or a story in the news?"

"Absolutely."

"And if it's a nice day, you feel bad about it, but if it's a bad day, you feel bad about that too."

"That's exactly how it is."

"Tell me, Brian, as you have been fighting with this, does the word 'depression' ever pop into your head."

"Sure."

"And does this make things worse because now you think you're sick?"

"Yes."

"You know, Brian," said Father Mike in a light-hearted tone of voice, "when most of us use the word 'depression,' we are not really thinking about a sickness." Brian was all ears now. "What we are talking about is tiredness, mental tiredness.

"The mind gets tired," continued Father Mike, "sometimes because of problems, but it doesn't take a problem. Just living, just living in the modern world, is tiring. There so much we have to think about and keep straight — stuff at work, stuff in relationships, dealing with money, maintaining a car. All of this takes energy and sometimes we run out.

"Then what happens?" This was not a question. "It's always the same. Whenever we are tired mentally, we always suffer the same symptom. Everything looks bad. Everything makes us feel bad. It is everything, but nothing. Almost everything produces fear. Our thoughts are out of control.

"All of this produces panic. People begin to scream, if only to themselves, 'What's wrong with me; what's wrong with me; will I ever get over this, will I ever feel good again?!'

"Naturally, this uses up more energy. This makes things look worse, causing us to panic all the more, using up more energy, making things look worse... and so it goes. We drive ourselves into a deep dark hole where we suffer very much *for nothing*. We suffer for nothing because we are taking ourselves most seriously at a time when we should be taking ourselves least seriously. After all, when we are tired, our mind — the thing that makes our judgments — is functioning most poorly.

"Is this making sense to you, Brian?"

"I think so."

"Stay with me a little longer."

Brian nodded.

Father Mike went on. "Now, to allow ourselves to rest and return to normal as quickly as possible, what we need to do is the following...." Here he paused for emphasis, to make sure that Brian was listening carefully.

"We need to recognize that when everything looks bad — including many things that never looked bad before—it's not everything; it's me; I'm *tired*. Therefore, at this time, I will not judge. I will not judge me. I will not judge my life or other people. I will try not to take my bad thoughts seriously."

"I think this is easier said than done," said Brian.

"I know it is," said Father Mike. "And it won't make us feel better immediately. After all, we are still tired. But knowing this helps us to understand why we feel bad. More importantly, it helps us not to make matters worse, and worse, and worse. Think about it, Brian—the treatment for exhaustion is not exercise!"

Brian smiled.

Father Mike went on. "When finally we begin to get rest, things will begin to look a little better. It will become a little clearer that this is how life works. We will get more rest. Things will now look even better. It will become even clearer that this is how life works. We will get even more sure about this once we've been through a few more of life's 'downs' *without making them worse*! And we will never be at the mercy of depression again."

"God...I mean...I wish that could be true."

"It is true, Brian. Just take your own feet off the fire. Just remember that when everything looks bad—including many things that never looked bad before—it's not everything, it's me; I'm tired."

"I feel a little better," said Brian.

"We've made a start, Brian," responded Father Mike, "but, please, please, be patient. There's one thing you have to watch out for. A little mental rest brings about an 'up.' This inspires hope, which uses energy, and brings us right back down. If instead we expect this to happen—and we *expect* the downs to make us wonder if we are really getting better—the downs will be less deep, and they will last for less time. The ups will be higher and longer. And, when we are up, we will see clearly that we really are on the way out.

"Am I making sense to you, Brian?"

"Yes," said Brian.

"Then explain it back to me." Father Mike was smiling—but he was serious.

Brian did a pretty good job.

"Good," said Father Mike, who gave Brian his guide to spiritual reading, a reflection, and an unusual object to put where he would often see it.

This was the reflection:

"THE SKYLINE"

The skyline of a city is a beautiful thing to see. But not always.

Some days, it does not look that good at all. There is pollution. There is humidity. There is something in the way.

Then there are other days. The winds clean the air and, especially at night, we see the city as if for the first time. We see buildings. We see windows in the buildings. We see how beautiful the city really is.

Herein lies the point. The fact is: what we see on a good day is what the city really looks like. After all, the buildings are always there. So are the windows.

On a really bad day, we don't see anything. This doesn't mean that the city isn't there. It means that it is a bad day — a day when we cannot see the city as it is.

We do well to keep this in mind the next time we take a look at ourselves. Sometimes it's just a bad day to look. We are tired. Something is bothering us. In any case, we are not in possession of our powers. We can know this because nothing looks good. Everything, however, cannot really be bad. It is us; probably we are tired; possibly we are upset. In any case, we don't have our powers. It is a bad day to look at anything.

Then there are good days. We have had rest. Nothing is presently going wrong. Our head is clear. Today we see well. Today we see things as they really are.

You are who you see on a good day. And you are never who you see on a bad one.

* * *

Dear Reader,

It has been this author's experience that the vast majority of people he talks to who are suffering from what they call depression are, in fact, suffering from mental tiredness, and understanding this helps them reverse the vicious circle described above. There are, however, times that understanding and trying to see things differently does not work. There are times when a person has a depression that requires medical help. If what we are talking about here does not begin to turn things around, please speak to a doctor about it; and please try not to think that the need to do so is some sort of failing. All of us need the expert help of many others to live well; and the different organs in our bodies are very fragile and often require special care. ∎

◘

EPILOGUE

Almost certainly you noticed that Father Mike gave almost all his visitors a guide to spiritual reading. This material is also available to you. Just visit the author's website at www.thefaithkit.org and click on "Read about how to use this site."

From this same site, if you click on "Check out The Faith Kit," you will find full-page versions of most of the materials that Father Mike gave the people who came to see him — and much, much more!

"The Skyline" that Father Mike gave Brian is available if you go back to the main page of thefaithkit.org and click on "Spiritual Diagnostics." Select "Depressed." Then, at the bottom of the reflection, click where it says "to read more."

You might be interested to know that when her second meeting was coming to an end, Luz brought up the case of a couple of friends who, as far as she could see, were having marriage problems. "I wish I could get them to talk to you," she said, "but I can't even mention that I think they're having problems." Father Mike asked a couple of questions about what Luz was seeing and then he suggested that she go to thefaithkit.org, click on "Panorama" and then click on "Gate 22." "If you like it," he said, "tell your friends you liked it and you thought they might like it. It's a diverse set of stories. It won't be obvious why you are suggesting it—except that you liked it. They'll notice the story that's meant for them."

"Gate 22" also includes a follow-up to the story of James!

If you found Father Mike to be an interesting character, you might like to take a look at his role in the spiritual novel *Kirk* which is also available from "Panorama."

Finally, in case you might be interested in knowing what Father Mike almost always suggests when people ask for a specific recommendation for spiritual reading, go back to "Panorama" and click on "MAD: a museum from the future." ■

You Might Also Like

Robert J. Cormier

Why We Look Up
Making Sense of Our Catholic Faith

Paperback, 144 pages, ISBN 978-08245-21202

People who want to understand what they believe will cherish these inspiring reflections — which offer proof that you don't need to be a theologian to have a rich faith that nourishes the heart and mind.

In the book's three parts, "Having Faith," "Living Faith," and "Practicing Faith," the award-winning author provides us with small gems for devotional reading and inspiration, on a wealth of questions that matter to us most, such as what suffering means, how to have a personal relationship with God, and the glory of Creation.

"Robert Cormier is a superb communicator. He makes faith come alive in words that people can understand. He makes you want a life of faith, and he shows you how to find it."

—Rev. Arthur Caliandro
Marble Collegiate Church, New York

*Support your local bookstore or order directly
from the publisher at www.CrossroadPublishing.com*

*To request a catalog or inquire about
quantity orders, please e-mail
sales@CrossroadPublishing.com*

The Crossroad Publishing Company

You Might Also Like

Robert J. Cormier

A Faith That Makes Sense
Reflections for Peace, Purpose, and Joy

Hardcover, 240 pages, ISBN 978-08245-18752

In this collection of brief reflections, Father Cormier takes elements common to many faiths and offers them in a way that can make sense to almost everyone. The simplicity and clarity of the reflections makes the texts easily accessible to a wide variety of readers. If read slowly and over time, they can inspire serious meditations.

"Written for those searching for faith, or those hoping to understand their faith more deeply, *A Faith That Makes Sense* takes the reader on a simple and optimistic journey. 'Share what faith has done for you,' we are urged. Robert Cormier takes his own advice and spells out what love, peace, and joy—as well as prayer, struggle, sacrifice, and so much more—amounts to, if understood in light of a faith made eminently sensible, and readable, in this insightful book."

—Rev. Dr. Paul A. Holmes, director
Toolbox for Pastoral Management, Seton Hall University

*Support your local bookstore or order directly
from the publisher at www.CrossroadPublishing.com*

*To request a catalog or inquire about
quantity orders, please e-mail
sales@CrossroadPublishing.com*

The Crossroad Publishing Company

You Might Also Like

Maria Boulding, OSB

Gateway to Hope
An Exploration of Failure

Paperback, 160 pages, ISBN 978-08245-26986

With each passage embracing human failure and loss, the elegant musings of Sister Maria Boulding speak gently and eloquently to those who set their goals high, yet struggle to grasp their own limitations and reconcile them with God, as well as to those who second guess their path in life, and to worshipers mourning the premature loss of friends and family. With each meditation on loss, Sister Boulding creates a spiritual, contemplative grid against which readers can interpret the setbacks of their life.

"[A] wonderful portrait of many failures throughout Scripture and how we all go through life dealing with the fear of failure and failure, itself. However, Boulding stresses that it is in failing that we come to realize how we can become successful."

— Rev. John Hogemann, OSB

Support your local bookstore or order directly
from the publisher at www.CrossroadPublishing.com

To request a catalog or inquire about
quantity orders, please e-mail
sales@CrossroadPublishing.com

The Crossroad Publishing Company

ABOUT THE AUTHOR

A priest of the Archdiocese of Newark, NJ, Robert J. Cormier is a preacher, teacher, theologian, and pilot.

For seventeen years, he led the Spanish-speaking community of St. Rose of Lima in Newark, a city he served for twenty-five years. During this time he ministered ten years to Portuguese-speaking communities and one year to an Italian-speaking community.

In addition, Father Bob has over twenty-five years' experience in both elementary and high schools, and over twenty years as both a prison chaplain and a rehab counselor. For the last eighteen years, he has been president of Project Live — a leading institution for the care of the mentally ill.

Between 1989 and 1998, he was one of the three voices of *The Radio Mass* once heard live throughout the Eastern seaboard. Currently he serves as the spiritual director of the Internet-based radio station Radio Inmaculada, on which he also airs a weekly program.

Father Bob has a pontifical license in philosophy from the Catholic University of America in Washington, DC, and a license in theology from the Gregorian University in Rome. He was ordained by Pope John Paul II in 1982.

He served as a deacon in Thailand, has visited some seventy other countries on six continents, and has some facility in eight modern languages. He spent fifteen summers as priest to the Mam, a Mayan tribe, in western Guatemala.

He is the creator of Christian Materialism, a strikingly new synthesis of philosophy and faith that comes complete with a spirituality, set of catechisms, books on marriage and ministry, works of fiction, music, and art, and more.

The combined tables of contents of his books and other writings and the catalog of his religious products include over two hundred pages.

Father Bob grew up in Cranford, NJ. Besides being a pilot, he is a mountain climber, sailor, cave explorer, scuba diver, and bus driver, and he plays the conga.

He currently is a member of the pastoral team that serves St. Patrick and Assumption/All Saints parishes in Jersey City. ■